Surprised by Agape

Second Edition

Justin Wiggins

Edited by Grant P Hudson

CLARENDON HOUSE PUBLICATIONS

www.clarendonhousebooks.com

Published by Clarendon House Publications
76 Coal Pit Lane, Sheffield, England

Published in Sheffield 2022

ISBN #: 9798355304027

'If I find in myself a desire which no experience in this world can satisfy, the most probable explanation is that I was made for another world.'
— C. S. Lewis

Justin Wiggins is an author who works and lives in the primitive, majestic, beautiful mountains of North Carolina. He graduated with his Bachelor's in English Literature from Montreat College with a focus on C. S. Lewis studies in May of 2018. His first book was *Surprised by Agape*, published by Grant Hudson of Clarendon House Publications; his second book, *Surprised By Myth*, co-written with Grant Hudson, was published in Autumn of 2021. His third and fourth books *Marty & Irene*, and *Tír na nÓg*, as well as his most recent fifth book, *Celtic Twilight*, were all published by Steve Cawte of Impspired in 2021 and 2022. He has also had poems, and other short pieces published by Clarendon House Publications, the C. S. Lewis Sehnsucht Journal, and by Sweetycat Press. Justin has a great zeal for life, work, community, writing, literature, art, pubs, bookstores, and coffee shops.

CONTENTS

Editor's Foreword 11
Introduction 15
Suicide, Rescue, Decisions and The Divine 19
Montreat College, Identity and Vocation 29
Interlude 39
Agape Love in the Writings of Lewis 41
The Power and Universality of Art 65
Surprised by Joy 71
Perelandra 75
The Weight of Glory 79
Till We Have Faces 83
C. S. Lewis and the Importance of Books 87
Visiting C. S. Lewis's Home The Kilns 91
The Legacy of George MacDonald 95
J. R. R. Tolkien 101
C. S. Lewis & Ireland 103
Conclusion 109
Annotated Bibliography 111
Further Bibliography 117

Editor's Foreword

Over the last five hundred years or so it is possible to see a trend in human civilisation in the West from the perception that the universe was an orderly, enclosed and relatively tranquil place, ruled over by a beneficent Providence, to a sense of the universe as being chaotic, open and violent, not ruled over by anything at all.

Some of the symptoms of this include the slow, apparently inevitable breakdown of what we now call 'organised religion' in the form of the Christian church, beginning with the church's own division into warring factions in the Reformation. Looking back on this change, it is possible to fall into the trap of what C. S. Lewis called 'chronological snobbery' and to believe that we, as people living in the 21st century, are somehow a natural and superior product of this collapse of 'religious prejudice' which took place painfully over several centuries and is still going on today, it seems. But that would be to deny the truth of what Lewis asserted, which was that the past was in reality no less wise than we. We use the term 'organised religion', but at the time in all likelihood things would have been perceived quite differently: the Church was not seen as a human institution at all, but as an extension of God's bodily presence upon Earth, managed by a direct line of anointed bishops from the time when Christ Himself walked among us. For over a thousand years, the general view was that we lived in a divinely created world, orbited by planets which were alive and in continuous worship of their Creator, under stars that shone with the light of the eternal Heaven which lay just beyond their sphere. The fact that human life was full of suffering and unpleasantries, war and death, was not a reflection upon the true state of things but an anomaly arising from Adam's sin in the Garden of Eden, a key moment of dysfunction which had thrown the whole of the Earth out of synchronisation with divine harmony. Individual souls suffered alone and collectively — that was part of existence. But they were redeemed and rewarded also, as part of that same existence — salvation was not denied them, but was built into the cosmic pattern.

Fast forward to today, and things have changed remarkably: the Church, seen very much as a human institution run by tragically fallible human beings, has declined in numbers and reputation; our world is no longer seen to be divinely created but exists as a result of a huge cosmic accident, and is orbited by planets which are fragments of spinning matter, under stars that are balls of burning gas too vast and too far away for our minds to apprehend. Human life is still full of suffering and unpleasantries, war and death, but many see this not as a moment of dysfunction but simply as an extension of a soulless existence which we share with the beasts from which we are said to have evolved. Individual souls suffer alone and collectively without hope of reward or redemption because the existential truth is that existence is empty of meaning: there is no cosmic pattern.

One of the interesting things about this cultural progression is the corresponding transformation of literature and art. In a divinely-ruled universe, art served God, as everything else did, and, like everything else, sought to imitate Him; as time went on and society changed, art became a thing in itself, ascribed to individuals, and seen as something that emerges from some kind of 'subconscious'. The faculty of human beings to imagine slowly moved from being perceived as divinely inspired to a kind of romantic urge, or the product of uprisings of beauty from an unknown, subjective source. Today, art and literature are bastions of assertive 'self-expression' and woe betide any who try to stand in their way, even while the audiences for artists shrink and fragment.

In the 20th century, as materialist philosophies commanded worldwide political movements and exploded into war, C. S. Lewis found himself physically, mentally and spiritually on the front line — serving in the First World War, he continued to battle against materialism between the wars and became the champion of a different kind of philosophy during the Second. Lewis discovered that one of the chief weapons that he could employ in this battle against meaninglessness was literature.

Lewis's journey from the accepted world view of his time towards another, older and arguably aesthetically richer view and how he found the tools to secure that progress for himself and others forms one of the most fascinating stories of his century. The fact that his journey impacted deeply on the lives of others is another kind of evidence of the shift in cultural consciousness and the fact that the contemporary vision of the nature of our cosmos leaves a gaping void in the hearts of many.

One such heart, seeking meaning, belongs to the author of this book. This is the tale of how Justin found meaning, discovered a way back towards an altogether different view of things, and walked down that path to find out where exactly it led. I think that Justin's journey will resonate with many who feel trapped in an empty universe and who feel that just behind an ordinary door may await a wholly divergent way of life.

Note on the Text: *Agape* is a Latin first name (and a word) from the Greek (*agapi*, with EE sound and the second syllable stressed: ah- GAH-pee).

—Grant P. Hudson

Introduction

My literary hero, the Irish scholar, C. S. Lewis, chose to call his conversion story from atheism to theism to Christianity, *Surprised by Joy*. I have chosen to call my own story *Surprised by Agape*. This is the story of how I came to embrace faith in Christ from agnosticism by asking philosophical questions, searching for meaning, personal experiences of pain, love, and joy, and by meeting people of other world views; it's the story of how I came to have an amazing diverse community of people in my life, and how I discovered a passion for literature.

This book has been a labor of love, and I hope people of different philosophies and cultural backgrounds can resonate with it in some meaningful way in the context of their own experience.

The Greek word *agape*, which is my favorite word from any language, means an unconditional and everlasting love. I have come to believe that The Creator has this kind love for all of humanity. Whether you believe in a loving Creator, in many gods, or in nothing spiritual or divine, what unites us all is that we are human beings with fears, hopes, dreams, personalities, and the desire to be loved. Each one of us has a unique and strange life narrative that is important, and we express this experience of being human through artistic storytelling.

I believe music, literature, film, painting, dance, and other artistic mediums of storytelling have a unique way of bringing people together and taking down barriers of social status, religion, and politics. From cave paintings in France to the Norse and Celtic myths, to the writings of C. S. Lewis, George MacDonald, J. R. R. Tolkien, Jane Austen, J. K. Rowling, John Keats, and including the *Lord of the Rings* films, pottery, painting, dance, and different genres of music — we all find something very meaningful to relate to through these art mediums. Art played a huge role in me embracing faith, and finding a passion that became a vocation. Pursuing this passion has brought me great joy, and has allowed me to have rich life experiences I absolutely marvel at.

One of those experiences was getting to go on a ten-day Oxford C. S. Lewis during my last semester of college before I graduated. I had never flown on a plane in my life, which is quite funny. I found the flight at first very terrifying, and then absolutely exhilarating as I looked in awe at the vast expanse below me. This trip to Oxford, England was life-changing for me. To get to see places associated with my favorite writer C. S. Lewis, his friend J. R. R. Tolkien and the other Inklings was quite epic. Seeing places like The Eagle and Child pub, Magdalen College, Addison's Walk, St. Mary The Virgin Church, Blackwell's bookshop, and Lewis's home The Kilns, was absolutely amazing. The beauty of Oxford was overwhelming, and I will remember that trip for the rest of my life. To this day I am still processing that experience.

One particular memory that really stands out vividly in my mind among many, was when I got to visit Lewis's grave.

When I was there I wept tears of joy, and said a prayer of gratitude to The Creator for giving the world such a humble, brilliant, Irish literary scholar and lay theologian. Lewis has had a profound impact on the man I am today. The same debt I owe to him can be likened to the debt that he owed to the Scottish fantasy writer George MacDonald. Both Lewis and MacDonald's lives were transformed by the Agape love of Christ, as was mine, and this is my story of how that happened. For me, this is what it means to be Surprised by Agape.

Thanks for taking the time to read my story. As I have said, I hope you can resonate with it in some meaningful way.

Shalom.

Introduction to the Second Edition:

My first book, *Surprised by Agape*, was published four years ago by the brilliant editor, writer, and publisher, Grant Hudson. I still marvel at how many people have connected with the book, all the reviews on Amazon and Goodreads, the moving endorsements from David Jack, Don King, and Carolyn Curtis, the video endorsement from Lewis's stepson Douglas Gresham, and being able to do a book signing at a local Barnes and Noble in Asheville, North Carolina. I owe a great debt to Grant Hudson of Clarendon House Publications for publishing the book. He made a dream of mine become a reality by publishing my first book, and I felt like I could honestly call myself a writer!

When I was writing *Surprised by* Agape, I honestly didn't know what I was doing, but I kept working hard, editing, revising, and I finished it! Writing a book is fun, but also hard work. I hope that you enjoy this expanded version. It includes a few chapters from *Surprised By Myth: Essays On The Inklings and Their Friends* which I co-wrote with Grant Hudson, that correlate with the agape love theme of the book, and one about Ireland and C. S. Lewis that is very dear to my heart. Lewis is my favorite writer, and Ireland is my favorite country that I have ever been to, so writing that particular chapter was very meaningful and brought back some rich memories.

—Justin Wiggins

Suicide, Rescue, Decisions
and The Divine

I was born in the state of North Carolina in the year 1989, and grew up in the country in a very small town called Deep Run, which is in eastern North Carolina. The countryside in Lenoir County is pleasant, beautiful, and serene, but there is also something very disturbing and oppressive about the atmosphere of Deep Run. Friends of mine who have grown up there have had the exact opposite experience and have found it very pleasant; my experience of it was like that of an innocent slave who yearned to be free while being held captive on a ship. Perhaps it has something to do with the terrible things that happened because of colonialism in America?

Deep Run was founded in 1925, and as painful as many of my memories are there, I still do have a fondness for it, as anyone has for the place they grew up in. I can still remember playing with the neighborhood kids, my Grandmother Marie's cooking, seeing fireflies in summer, the smell of hog farms, cut grass, and the neighborhood racket of diesel trucks; watching *The Simpsons*, *The Fresh Prince of Bel Air*, movies that I was not supposed to watch but got away with by being clever, and reading books like *Where the Red Fern Grows* and *The Giving Tree.* Yet I longed to move away from the area, and indeed I did that when I had the chance later in my teens.

I didn't grow up in dire poverty, nor did I grow up lavishly rich. I suppose my life would be called 'middle class.' I was raised by a loving family, mostly by women — my aunts, my mother, and my dear Nana (the most loving person I have ever known in my life). There were some very good male figures like my uncle, a few cousins, and my grandfather. Yet the deepest wound would be the absence of my father, which caused philosophical confusion and an unhealthy self-loathing. My father was around some when I was young, but there was this repeated pattern of him disappearing and reappearing because of his battle with drug addiction. He eventually became completely absent from my life when I was a teenager, and this would create a fear in me of being abandoned by people whom I loved, and cause me to be quite skeptical of a good and loving Creator that cared about all his children.

To make matters worse, the cultural Christianity that I grew up with in Lenoir county left a bad taste in my mouth. There were certainly sincere and devout people, and I am thankful that my family taught me the virtues of faith, hope, and love, but the whole cultural fundamentalism planted ideas in my mind that were very hard to counter — rapture theology, a morbid obsession with heaven and hell, and a western evangelical interpretation of Christianity, which is very different from how Christianity began in the first century. It is so easy for any worldview to be distorted by those who use it for their own agenda! I sincerely believed that all Christians then viewed everything through the particular flimsy theological spectacles that I wore.

Well, those spectacles cracked when I started to ask questions, and discovered that I had no idea why I believed what I believed. Everything that I was taught was from a Southern Free Will Baptist perspective. This was all that I knew and lived with during my elementary and high school years. I know many people do not have a negative experience with this particular denomination, but I did. My curiosity and horror at feeling lost in the cosmos, and having a suspicion that what I was being taught was just cultural and therefore a delusion, brought me to a crisis in my life. With the emptiness that was building up, I tried to find meaning in praying, reading the Bible, being part of a church community, listening to Christian music, going to youth group trips, door knocking, witnessing, and growing in my salvation. I thought this was all a good moral and cultural thing to do, and I did find some satisfaction in it. Yet I reached a point where I couldn't fabricate this cultural religion any longer, and in due time, from father abandonment issues, struggles with depression, and having no answers to all of these philosophical questions, I found myself in a really dark place. I was scared as hell of the possibility of being alone in the cosmos. I didn't understand anything about science, philosophy, the cultural and theological importance of myth, Buddhism, Hinduism, Islam, Judaism, how diverse Christianity was, or other worldviews for that matter. A geographical location has a profound impact on your perspective. Every time I go back and visit family and friends in the area I grew up in, a melancholy comes over me that is linked to so many of my memories. Yes, I had good times that still bring a smile to my face, and sometimes tears of joy to my eyes, yet most of my memories are full of sadness, loss, confusion, and emptiness. All of this is connected to the philosophical confusion I did not know how to even articulate to people at that time in my life.

It could have been worse, of course. I could have grown up in a religious cult that uses brainwashing to breed hate, bigotry, racism, and an 'us vs. them' mentality. I suppose I was meant to go through these experiences which would lead up to the revolutionary time in my life when I came to understand who I was as Justin Wiggins, and what I was created to do.

So, how did faith become a virtue to me?

It started with music. Music became a healing experience for me, which opened up my mind and heart in a way that nothing else really did. For me, it was a particular rock band called Switchfoot. In discovering the music of Switchfoot, I was able to start articulating questions, and to realize that it was okay to ask questions, and that I was not alone. Their songs helped me through really dark seasons of depression and identity crisis experiences. I can still remember the joy I felt when I went to my first concert and saw Switchfoot play a show in Winston Salem with Relient K on their Habitat for Humanity Tour in 2007. It was my first time driving such a distance, and although I was really messed up at that time in my life, I cherished every single moment of that night. Even now, I can still remember hearing songs like Meant to Live, Dare You to Move, Stars, Awakening, and the people I talked with, how cold it was, and the intimate after-show that Jon

Foreman played at a small coffee shop that no longer exists. This would be the beginning of a new chapter in my life. In this chapter I would experience such a depth of pain that it almost destroyed me, find a great love for literature and art, and embrace faith.

Embracing faith was the most important decision that I ever made in my life. It changed the way I loved and appreciated the people in my life, how I spent my money, my time, how my interest and passion for literature, music, and art developed, the way I lived my life on an everyday basis — and my brain chemistry. This experience was a supernatural encounter with The Creator of the universe. How else could I explain it? I couldn't find any logical way. Is this not the case with different experiences people have?

The closest thing we have as human beings when it comes to expressing the inexpressible is artistic storytelling. The moment I finally came to understand why storytelling is important to us was when I read Lewis's *The Chronicles of Narnia*. I still have the copy I bought about ten years ago from a Barnes and Noble in Greenville, North Carolina — it was *The Magician's Nephew* in particular that moved me profoundly. It was the creation story that helped me understand why stories have been important to us human beings since the beginning. I also finally understood why Jesus of Nazareth told parables in the first century to communicate things about the kingdom of heaven to people from all walks of life. That experience of reading the creation story is quite hard to put into logical language. I could not find the words then, when the experience was new to me. It was my first experience of the transcendent.

Whether you believe the transcendent is merely a chemical reaction going on in the brain, or something spiritual, it is still part of our human history, written about prolifically by philosophers and psychologists in order to understand its relation to human consciousness. This first important spiritual experience I can vividly remember, for me, began my search and longing to know who I was created to be as Justin Wiggins.

After reading the Narnia stories, I got a copy of Lewis's *Mere Christianity*. Reading that book was a very important experience for me. It helped me understand Christianity, different worldviews, language, and what it means to embrace faith. It is incredible to me that this book was originally a series of BBC radio broadcasts during the Second World War, and that it is still one of the bestselling books on spirituality. From that point on, I began to read anything I could get my hands on by Lewis.

After my conversion to Christianity from Agnosticism, I went to a local community college in Winterville, North Carolina, called Pitt Community College to get my two-year liberal arts degree. During this period of my life, I found friends that spoke my language, which was an absolute delight. I was thankful to be able to share my passion for music, books, film, literature, philosophy, history, and mythology with these incredible individuals. I would meet these people by going to the local Starbucks, Barnes and Noble, pubs, church, and through other friends. Through getting to know them I found encouragement, a common bond in faith, and a strengthening of friendship. This was the same camaraderie that the Inklings shared together, and was something I had longed for, for so long. Gone were the days of feeling terribly alone, being so bored out of my mind that I would play basketball and yahoo checkers just to pass the time and to try and not face the emptiness that kept growing within. With these friends, I spent many golden hours talking about faith, how our day was, what our struggles and questions were, our favorite movies, writers, and anything else under the sun. These friends were also there for me when I would be struggling, feeling confused and stuck. The Greeks called the gift of friendship *Philia*, and it is one of the supreme joys of this life.

Pain is something that is universally experienced. It is one reason why spirituality and art exist — we long to find answers to this problem of suffering and evil that has plagued us since the beginning of time. Pain can strengthen what you believe, or it can leave you cynical and jaded. I never thought that I would ever get to such a point to where I did not want to exist anymore. Yet it did happen, and it shook the very foundations of my being and almost destroyed me — at that point in my life I wished it would have.

The build-up to my suicide attempts was very gradual. Years and years of suppressed father abandonment issues, and flopping out of the university I was going to because of horrific struggles with depression, came together, and I just found it to be unbearable. So how did I respond to this all of this? I contemplated the easiest and least violent way to die, and I came to the conclusion that taking sleeping pills would be the easiest.

I remember very vividly going to a Target store in Greenville, North Carolina, and purchasing sleeping pills with the hope that they would kill me. I did not succeed in killing myself, but my suicide attempt did not end well. During those really dark days, out of curiosity I would look up how different artists had killed themselves, and weep thinking that all of those beautiful people ended up dying tragically, while wondering if The Creator really cared about all of them. In this context, how does one make sense of the verse from The Bible that gets trumpeted a lot, 'I will never leave you nor forsake you'? Does the Creator really care about us? I thought. Pain raises the question how can a good Creator allow such suffering? Every individual that is honest with themselves asks this question. It is something that I wrestle with quite a lot, as do many people of different worldviews.

Lewis tried to approach this question very honestly in his book *The Problem of Pain*, published in 1940, and also in his book *A Grief Observed*, which was published under the pseudonym N. W. Clerk, after losing his wife Joy Davidman to cancer. Posing this question to myself has provided good writing, has strengthened my faith, and has allowed me to help people who have had similar struggles, which has brought me joy. Yet, when I was in the crisis in my life, I had no reason to live, and found myself being angry towards The Creator for bringing me into being without my consent. I didn't understand why I lived everyday with the desire to not live. Why did I get to that point? Was my faith just a human fabrication? Was I going to make it? How did I go from being so passionate about life to believing that it was a curse to be a conscious human being on this planet? Those were questions that I posed to myself that kept me up at night, and that I had no answers for. Yet, I could not ignore how the Divine pervaded everything, even in the darkness that I was in. I could not deny how The Creator changed my life by the power of His love. It would be easy to say that it was all just chance, and that I was duped into believing in something that did not exist because I found Christianity to be a beautiful story of redemption, but simply a story, and nothing more. Sometimes that kind of skepticism can creep in and convince one that faith is, like Bram Stoker stated in his classic novel *Dracula*, 'that faculty which enables us to believe things which we know to be untrue.' Some people embrace this view with delight, and some with reluctance because they want to believe in a good Creator or some spiritual worldview that will give their life meaning.

As for me, I came very close indeed to embracing this kind of worldview. Yet, I did not. As I write these words and look back on that dark, strange time in my life, I sincerely marvel that I continued to believe in Christ and didn't become cynical. Why? Because I am inquisitive, I ask questions, and I would be the last person to embrace a worldview because someone told me it was true, or because I grew up culturally assimilated to a particular religion. I could have been a Hindu living in India that became a Buddhist. I could have been a Christian that converted to a pagan earth-based religion, or Islam. I could have been a Christian that became an atheist or an agnostic under the influence of Bertrand Russell, Christopher Hitchens, Lucretius, or even Monty Python. Yet, through the influence of the musician Jon

Foreman, and the writers C. S. Lewis and George Mac-Donald, I bowed the knee to Christ, and found Him to be the same Jesus of faith and history. Conversions are fascinating in that they completely change someone's intellect, imagination, personality, desires, and give life meaning.

Montreat College, Identity and Vocation

I still remember when I first got my acceptance letter into East Carolina University, which is in Greenville, North Carolina. I had my doubts about being able to get two-year liberal arts degree from Pitt Community College because of a wretched math class that I believed I was going to flunk. Doing math, to me, was like someone asking me to translate Egyptian hieroglyphics into English! It was the last class that I had to take (I wished it would have been a literature course), and with many frustrating moments of cursing, feeling defeated, seeking encouragement from friends, and studying very hard by having numerous cups of coffee, and listening to a Spotify playlist to help me through purgatory, I passed the class with a C and made it! It was the last step before being accepted into ECU.

ECU was founded in 1907, and is known as one of the world's largest partying schools in the States. Nonetheless, the campus is beautiful, and the university has great business, nursing, medicine, science, literature, and other disciplinary studies. I was very proud of myself for making it that far, and for moving on beyond community college to this university where I could pursue my passion for literature. I still remember the joy of living on ECU's campus, the joy I found in the classes on literature I took, and the joy I felt experiencing a university atmosphere and pursuing my passion.

As with life, though, things happened in Greenville that I did not ever think were possible. In my second semester, I gradually slipped into such a low depression that I found existence to be a nightmare. This was something beyond anything I had experienced before, so I found it very unsettling. I can still vividly remember the days that I wanted to get out of bed, but found that I couldn't. Soon I found myself not being able to make it to class, flunking important tests, having a bizarre sleeping pattern, and contemplating different ways of ending my life. In this state of being, I asked myself why people chose to end their lives, and what if I had been lying to myself by claiming to believe that there was a good, loving God that cared about human beings?

During these dark days of depression at East Carolina University, one of my very good friends took the time out of his busy schedule to drive to Greenville, pick me up, and take me out for a pint and a good meal — and it was just what I needed. I was still in a terribly dark place, but that act of kindness and love from a true friend gave me some sort of hope to hold onto. I was horrified at the fact that I had cursed so many of my friends out, told them that their prayers were in vain, and that they worshipped a celestial dictator that did not exist. I can still remember looking a friend of mine in the face that I went to apologize to on ECU's campus. He forgave me, but told me I had crossed some lines when I had said, 'Fuck Christianity' to him. I had never been so angry in my life. Years later this friend was to forgive me, and we were reconciled, which brought me joy. He showed me Agape love lived out when I did not deserve it.

The next few years would be very difficult. I had moved back home to the town I hated, and worked a job that I felt was meaningless. This was a very strange time. Issues like depression, anxiety, bipolar disorder, and other forms of mental illness are quite complex. This whole time I could not function or sit still, and found it hard to read or convey things in a logical way. I went to see many counselors and doctors, tried different medications and therapy. All of this did of course help some in regard to healing, but I was still having such horrific lows that I did not want to be there anymore. I thought I was going to eventually succumb to madness. Looking back over all of that hell, I should not have made it. I should not be here. Yet, I did make it; I am here. Was this by chance, or was it by grace?

Depression is a form of mental illness, and is something I have struggled with, and will be something I struggle with for the rest of my life. Many great writers, and many individuals I know have struggled with this as well. I have never seen a burning bush, the dead raised, someone healed of cancer, dementia, or blindness. I have never experienced a full healing from depression. Yet, through counseling, doctors, medication, community, love, comedy, and art, I have experienced healing. This is where the Fatherhood of the Creator has been central to my faith. My subjective feelings come and go, but my identity as Justin Wiggins in the Creator remains constant.

Things did get better when I eventually got a job as a barista. It got me out of the atmosphere of the grocery store job that I hated, and I was able to do work that I enjoyed which also paid my bills. I loved making lattes, cappuccinos, smoothies, different drinks, and talking with people from all walks of life. I did find some meaning in the job, yet I was still restless, and I still felt quite sick and lost. I grew weary from just talking about going back to college.

In 2015 things took an interesting turn in my life when I was invited to an Inklings retreat in the mountains of North Carolina at Montreat College, which is right outside of Black Mountain. I had never been to the mountains of North Carolina in my life, and when I first came there, I found them enchanting.

I attended the C. S. Lewis Inklings retreat which was in honor of Lewis's wife, Joy Davidman's birthday. The guest speaker was Lewis and Tolkien scholar, Colin Duriez. At this retreat I loved meeting all of the wonderful people who were kindred spirits, and the seed was planted in my life for coming to Montreat College in the future. Two very important experiences happened there. One was that I met Lewis scholar, teacher, and writer Dr. Don King, and Lewis and Tolkien scholar Colin Duriez. I was very intimidated when I met both men, but they made me feel right at ease once the conversation started. At the time, I had no idea that a year and a half later Colin and his wife Cindy Zudys would be giving me a tour around Oxford, England!

About a year after the Inklings retreat, I was working a barista job at Books A Million in New Bern, North Carolina. I knew I could not do barista work as a career, and that if I wanted to fully experience the joy of the vocation I was called to, I would have to finish my bachelor's degree in literature. A new chapter in my life started when I reached out to Don King, filled out an application to go to Montreat College, and got accepted. As comical as it sounds, I was quite nervous about moving five hours away from where I was living. Yet, by taking that risk, I would have rich life experiences that I absolutely marvel at now. When I first moved to Montreat, it took some time to get used to driving in the mountains, the funky, esoteric, strange and charming culture of Asheville, and to call this beautiful part of North Carolina, my 'shire'. I finally got to that point, and I now gladly called the mountains of North Carolina home.

My time here has been very rich indeed. I had the opportunity to meet C. S. Lewis scholar and pastor Jerry Root when he came from Wheaton College in Illinois for a conference at Montreat College. Jerry took the time out of his schedule to join me at the local coffee shop in downtown Black Mountain called the Dripolator. We enjoyed good coffee, pipe tobacco, and shared our stories with one another. Jerry is a very wise man, loves to listen to people, and pours so much into people.

I also had the honor to meet Lewis's stepson Douglas Gresham when he came for a conference in Black Mountain at the Created Institute. Meeting the step-son of Lewis and the son of Joy Davidman was something I had always wanted to experience, and getting to be in the same room with him, hear him talk about his memories of the love he witnessed between his mother and Jack Lewis, and his memories of The Inklings, was quite amazing. I highly recommend his book *Lenten Lands My Childhood with Joy Davidman and C. S. Lewis.*

In May 2018, I graduated with my bachelor's in literature from Montreat College, and I will remember that moving ceremony for the rest of my life. Things in my life would have turned out quite different if I had graduated from East Carolina University. The Creator had a different plan for my life. 'All things work together for the good of those who love God' says St. Paul in Romans 8, which was written between 50 and 60. A.D. I have found that to be true in my life. Out of so much suffering, came so much beauty and joy in my life — coming to Montreat College, going on an Oxford trip, my last semester, the amazing community of people that came into my life, and graduating with my bachelor's in literature.

There have been many biographies, essays, and reviews written about Lewis. In my attempt to convey his profound impact on my faith, I fear my words can seem repetitive. Yet *Surprised by Agape* is my own story, and I write about Lewis with the conviction that it will be appreciated by many people whose lives have also been impacted by him.

Why did I find Lewis's writings so revolutionary? There are numerous reasons I can give, but I will just describe a few. One particular reason is that Lewis lived out what he believed. Faith to him was not something you did in your private life, but something that encompassed all of life. To go from being an atheist in the tradition of David Hume, Bertrand Russell, and Lucretius, to becoming a follower of Jesus of Nazareth, is quite a miracle. It would be easy to write Lewis's conversion off as wishful thinking, but that would be absurd, because he was a man who had had a philosophical education and who knew how to think critically.

Lewis was not a trained theologian, but a scholar of literature, which, in my opinion, makes his work more accessible in communicating important things about spirituality, morality, art, and life experience in layman's terms. Many theologians, philosophers, and historians have written some important works that have stood the test of time, but I think Lewis was able to reach a wider audience because he had an incredible imagination, and knew how to weave a story with underlying Christian themes. That combination is quite unique. Two really great examples of this, are his two works of fiction *The Screwtape Letters* and *The Great Divorce*. *The Screwtape Letters* gave Lewis great popularity as a religious writer, which many of his colleagues greatly resented and criticized. *The Great Divorce* is an imaginative book about the importance of human decisions in the context of eternity. These two works by Lewis have been read and re-read by thousands of people around the world who are of very different worldviews and cultural backgrounds. I find them to be universal and amazing approaches to apologetics, and not weak in anyway. Perhaps I have a bias because I have such a strong emotional attachment to Lewis's works as they have impacted my life in a profound way, but, speaking from my own experience as a reader and a writer, I find his theological and spiritual works, and his works of fiction and apologetics to be very challenging, engaging, moving, and spiritually nourishing. Apologetics is very interesting to me, and I believe that it certainly clears intellectual barriers, and helps people with questions they have about the Christian faith, but it can become very dry, rationalistic, and also seem arrogant with its claims and exclusivity. Yet at the same time, aren't all worldview claims exclusive? C. S. Lewis explores that in many of his works, and though he does believe that Christianity is true, he had still quite an open theology. There are particular passages from *Mere Christianity*, *The Last Battle*, and from many of his other works and letters which suggest the inclusive view that he had, which I don't believe to be in contradiction to orthodox Christianity.

Because Lewis was an atheist for so long before becoming a devout Christian and Anglican, it gave him an understanding of different worldviews that he could have had in no other way. In the 1920s and 30s the psychological materialism of Sigmund Freud, the philosophy of Bertrand Russell, David Hume, and Frederic Nietzsche dominated many intellectual circles throughout the U. K. It seemed as though Christianity and all other religions were outdated and shown to be embarrassing and nothing but wish-fulfilment. I am certain that Lewis had his own moments when he wished he could go back to being an atheist, to not being 'interfered with', but, he knew that would be a lie, and intellectually dishonest. In the end, interestingly enough, it was not argument, philosophy, history or theology that brought him to faith (though they had their place) but it was an innate yearning and longing for The Creator that he knew that was not just a chemical reaction going on in the body.

In this post-modern pluralist age, storytelling has become an incredible way of conveying the beauty and the hope of the Gospel. For example, C. S. Lewis's Narnia books, his Space Trilogy, and J. R. R. Tolkien's *The Hobbit*, *The Silmarillion*, and *The Lord of the Rings* are still being read and re-read. The film industry has used these mythical works of literature in their own way to convey Christian truths, even if they did not intend to. The faith of Tolkien and Lewis certainly shows strongly through their incredible works of fiction. I think this is evidence that, although theological, historical and philosophical works by writers such as N. T. Wright and others have certainly made a powerful impact, storytelling seems to be a very powerful way of reaching a vast audience in this post-modern world.

Interlude

During my last semester at Montreat College I chose to write about Agape love in the writings of Lewis for my senior thesis, and about *Sehnsucht* in the writings of Lewis for the Oxford trip. In these two research papers that were required, I tried to give a context of why I thought these themes were important in understanding Lewis's worldview, why he is such a renowned writer worldwide, and how much his writings have meant to me on my journey of faith. I have included material from these two papers in the chapters of this book because I believe they bring the narrative together in a logical, coherent way. I did hours and hours of research, writing and editing, and received constructive criticism from my friend and C. S. Lewis scholar Dr. Don King. Finishing these two research projects helped me grow as a writer, gave a greater passion for literature, the writings of MacDonald and Lewis, and reminded me of why I do what I do.

Agape Love
in the Writings of Lewis

The Irish literary scholarly, lay theologian, and Christian apologist C. S. Lewis gave the world some of the most important works ever written on Christianity. Before Lewis's conversion in 1931, he had nothing to say and had failed as a poet according to the standards of the literary culture at the time. Yet, after he came to know Christ through intellectual and historical questions, and mystical experiences of joy through literature, art, and landscape, he found that he had something to say that he believed was so important that it had eternal consequences. That something was that humankind is not alone in the cosmos, and that The Creator loved humanity so much that He came to dwell as a Rabbi on this earth in the first century, suffered a horrific death by the Romans, and rose gloriously three days later, defeating death and offering hope and redemption to everyone.

The Greek word for this depth of love is *agape*. It means unconditional and everlasting love. I believe that this is the most important theme in the writings of Lewis. Without his personal experience of the Agape Love of Christ, he would not have been the man and writer that he was. Through coming to know Christ, Lewis found his true identity and vocation as a writer and scholar. In this chapter, I shall be exploring the theme of Agape love in Lewis's *The Four Loves*,

George MacDonald: An Anthology, *Mere Christianity*, and *A Grief Observed*. Why? Because I believe these four particular books uniquely display how Lewis's theological understanding of *agape* love developed in his life.

After coming to know Christ, Lewis found his voice and was able to write prolifically. The way Christ drew Lewis to himself, how he came to experience *agape* love, and how Lewis found out who he was created to be and what he was created to do is quite a fascinating and unique story. Inklings scholar and writer Colin Duriez writes in his book *Lewis A Biography of Friendship*:

The Gospel accounts were (as he learned through Tolkien) the highest point of human storytelling and myth-making, with an astounding dimension of historical veracity. Everything was true in the actual, primary world, without losing the quality of myth that engendered Joy. (p133).

What was once to Lewis a worldview that he saw as wishful thinking became something that gave his life meaning. This something was more powerful than any theological, philosophical, or historical argument, greater than any of the writers he had read, his pride, and anything that humanity has achieved in the thousands of years that we have been on this earth — it was the Agape Love of God.

The God of Love who created the world, nature, human beings, and the love that made it possible for humanity to be redeemed after we had broken a sacred covenant in the very beginning is the same God that pursued Lewis relentlessly.

Before redemption became a reality for Lewis, it was all dull religious platitudes. He had heard all the rhetoric growing up a Protestant in North Ireland about the love of Christ, but it was nothing more than a normal cultural thing. In *Surprised by Joy*, Lewis stated that he did not find much interest in his religious upbringing. Another example would be when Lewis committed the sin of taking communion when he was still an atheist. When it became real in his life, it would change everything forever.

I chose *The Four Loves* first, because Lewis writes poignantly about how family love, affection, romantic love, and charity are gifts from The Creator that reflect *agape* love in the context of human experience, and yet also how they need to be redeemed from becoming idols, because of our fallen human nature.

The second book, *Mere Christianity*, I chose because it has been one of the most important works of Christian apologetics ever written about how fallen we are as human beings, and yet how much Christ loves humanity.

The third book, *George MacDonald: An Anthology*, I chose because MacDonald influenced Lewis's understanding of the love of God many years before his conversion from atheism to Christianity, and would become his favorite writer. The fact that he took the time to compile the anthology and published it in 1946, speaks volumes about the profound influence MacDonald's theology had on Lewis's understanding of *agape* love.

The fourth book, *A Grief Observed*, I chose because this book captures how the *agape* love of Christ sustained Lewis through heartbreaking grief after he sadly lost his wife Joy Davidman to bone cancer.

The Agape Love of Christ can be seen in many of Lewis's other fascinating works, as we will see, but I believe these four particular books by him uniquely show his understanding, by experience, of how amazing the Agape love of Christ is for humanity.

War, Trauma and Agape Love

During the hell of the First World War, Lewis found himself asking the philosophical question about how can a loving God allow such evil when he was at the front lines of the war in France on his nineteenth birthday.

Although Lewis grew up as a Protestant in Northern Ireland, he had eventually come to the conclusion that all religions, including Christianity, were man-made attempts to seek to answer questions about sin, death, love, and the afterlife. Though he respected religion's honest attempt at trying to understand the universe, and greatly appreciated religious writers like G. K. Chesterton, George MacDonald, Virgil, and George Herbert, Lewis still found their religious claims erroneous.

Under the influence of his tutor William Kirkpatrick, Lewis's atheism had hardened. He had read all the first anti-theistic writers like Epicurus, Lucretius and Democritus, and also more contemporary atheist writers in his day like David Hume, H. G. Wells and Bertrand Russell. These brilliant writers all wrote in their own unique voice, but at the heart of their writings was the same argument that if there was a good and loving God, the world would not be in such a horrific state.

In his book *The Oxford Inklings,* scholar Colin Duriez writes about Lewis's philosophical experience of being trained under Kirkpatrick:

Lewis was not content until Albert [Lewis's father] entrusted his son to a private tutor named William T. Kirkpatrick, based in Bookham in Surrey. Lewis called him 'The Great Knock' because of the sheer force of his intellectual rigor. (p61)

It took Lewis many years to finally see a problem with the atheistic view that religious experience began with human beings trying to console themselves of the fear of death, and to experience the Love of God that pursued him so relentlessly. The great English poet Francis Thompson describes God as 'The Hound of Heaven' in his relentless pursuit of him in his brokenness and sin. Towards the end of Lewis's *Surprised by Joy,* he refers to himself as a fox being hunted by God, terrified that he might end up being caught. In the year 1929, Lewis, after many years of resistance, came to finally believe that there was a God, and became a theist.

Eventually Lewis found that he could not remain just a theist, even as comfortable as that position was. A theistic God is not active in the world, and so there are no demands made at all upon an individual. Finally, in 1931, Lewis came to a place of surrender and then became a Christian. This experience completely transformed his worldview, and as a writer, he finally had something to say. Lewis found that his pride, lust, chronological snobbery, and worldly desire to become a great poet would never satisfy the great yearning for joy and to know what it meant to be himself as Clive Staples Lewis.

After his conversion, Lewis wrote prolifically. He wrote literary criticism, fairy tales for children, poetry, popular theological works, a science fiction trilogy, other works of fiction, essays, and answered a vast number of letters.

The Four Loves

The Four Loves was published in 1960, towards the end of Lewis's life.

As mentioned, from the Greek language, the highest form of love is *agape* love, a love that is eternal, and utterly selfless. This word was used in the early Christian church in the first century and is used approximately 320 times in the New Testament to convey, in human language, God's love for humanity. Lewis had found that he could not run away from the Agape love of Christ. He had tried and failed to hide behind the chronological snobbery, or the spirit of age, which included the claim that religion and spirituality was a phenomenon of the past, and that what was good to believe was the predominant philosophy that truth can be verified empirically (*The Oxford Inklings* p71).

One of the most important chapters from Lewis's *The Four Loves* is the one on *philia*, which is Greek for friendship. Friendship between males (and between females) reflects the glory, beauty and Agape love of God. As stated before,

Lewis's friendships were very important to him. Perhaps his closest friend from this literary group was the philologist and author of *The Lord of the Rings,* J. R. R. Tolkien. Tolkien showed Lewis what the love of Christ looked like lived out, helping to bring Lewis to faith at a time in his life when he was very resistant to the Christian faith. Though they had very strong disagreements because of the differences in Protestant and Catholic theology, they both were able to give one another great encouragement in finishing their books.

There have been a lot of inaccurate things written in print about how Lewis and Tolkien were estranged later in their lives because of theological differences, Lewis's marriage to Joy Davidman, a suspicion that Tolkien was envious of how prolific Jack was, and that he did not approve of Jack being a lay theologian (since that was not his area of expertise). However, the evidence for this estrangement is very scanty. According to Inkling scholar Colin Duriez, though the friendship somewhat cooled, there was still the great bond that had once been there:

He (Tolkien) acknowledged that without the encouragement of Lewis, he never would have completed the task of many years' duration... (p180).

It would be three friends in particular that would show the atheist Jack Lewis the fallacy of contemporary thought. The lawyer, poet, and anthroposophist Owen Barfield, the writer, professor, and philologist J. R. R. Tolkien, and the writer Hugo Dyson, would all help Lewis understand many things that he could not from his own narrow paradigm. The particular lie that Lewis had bought into was that though myths were moving, and religion was an interesting and early failed attempt to provide our primitive ancestors with answers to important questions, all of it was simply human fabrication with absolutely no evidence. Dyson, Barfield, and Tolkien pointed out to Lewis that the origin of human consciousness, language, art, and the very beginning of myth and spiritual experience has a divine origin rather than a materialistic one. They all argued that the divine explanation was more logical and beautiful, and the material one was one for which there was no evidence but only assumptions. (*The Oxford Inklings* p72*)*. This was a great revelation to Lewis, and influenced his leap from atheism to theism. But in terms of the later book *The Four Loves*, these friendships of Lewis's are a great example of how *philia* reflects the Agape Love of God for humanity.

Lewis, Tolkien, Barfield, Dyson, Warren Lewis, and Charles Williams would all meet in Lewis's rooms at Magdalen College and The Eagle and Child pub in Oxford to read aloud their works, talk nonsense, theology, literature, and life experience over beer, tea, cider and pipe tobacco.

Lewis's brother Warren Lewis describes what the camaraderie was like between the Inklings in a foreword he wrote to a volume of Lewis's collected letters:

The ritual of an Inklings meeting was unvarying. When half a dozen or so had arrived, tea would be produced, and then when pipes were alight Jack would say, 'Well, has nobody got anything to read us?' To read to the Inklings was a formidable ordeal, and I can still remember the fear with which I offered the first chapter of my first book — and my delight, too, at its reception (p33).

As mentioned, without Lewis's encouragement Tolkien would have never finished his masterpiece *The Lord of the Rings,* and it could be argued that Lewis would have never become a Christian without Tolkien. It is amusing and charming that Lewis's dedicated his book *The Screwtape Letters* to J. R. R. Tolkien. Lewis and Tolkien both met for the first time over tea in 1926, and their friendship ended with Lewis's sad death in 1963, on coincidentally the same day that the writer Aldous Huxley died, and President John F. Kennedy was shot.

In the Christian worldview, family love, affection, the love between friends, and romantic love reflects the glory, beauty, and Agape Love of Christ. These loves are sacred gifts from The Creator, but they can become distorted, twisted, and idolatrous. In the introduction Lewis references the verse from Scripture which says 'God is love.' Then Lewis makes a distinction between 'gift-love' and 'need-love'. An example of gift-love would be an individual who has a gift of being a writer, musician, doctor, teacher, mother, or father, and who glorifies God with it. An example of need-love would be an individual needing a community of people intellectually, emotionally, physically, and spiritually.

An important relationship in Lewis's life that portrays this innate human need for community was his friendship with Arthur Greeves. They first bonded over a common interest in Norse mythology. Throughout their lives, they would confide to each other their secrets, and be the true definition of genuine friends.

In the Bible, *The Song of Solomon* is an allegorical poem that represents the Lover and the Beloved. This symbolizes not only Eros, erotic love, but also the Agape love that The Creator has for humanity. In the chapter on Eros, Lewis points out how romantic love can be possessive and therefore a sin (p138). This love, like friendship and affection, needs redemption. Lewis makes the distinction between carnal possessiveness and pure romantic love by saying, 'Sexual desire, without Eros, wants it, the thing in itself. Eros wants the beloved' (p120-121).

Mere Christianity

In the 1940s, Lewis was invited by James Welch to give radio lectures over the BBC during the Second World War. Welch had read Lewis's *The Problem of Pain,* and believed that Lewis would be a good choice in trying to bring hope to the people of England during the dark days of the war. These radio broadcasts would eventually become the best-selling theological work *Mere Christianity.* This book is a great example of Lewis being able to communicate profound theological and philosophical things in a way that everyone could understand. Along with conveying theology into the vernacular, Lewis sincerely believed it was his duty as a Christian to communicate the Agape love of God to a nation that was at war.

It is quite ironic, considering the fact that Lewis once believed all religions to be man-made, that at that time he was the most popular Christian writer of his day. This did end up costing him, especially at Oxford where he was never offered a chair like he was at Magdalen College, Cambridge, later on in his career. Many of Lewis's colleagues also thought that he had no business writing popular books on theology because he was not a trained theologian. Even with this criticism, Lewis did what he felt was his duty as a lay theologian. Because he did this, he was able to help many people who had serious doubts and questions about suffering, pain, and whether or not there really was a good and loving God.

In trying to convey the love of God, Lewis believed it was necessary to recover a sense of guilt, which in Christianity is the doctrine of original sin. He believed that the secular age that he was living in, influenced by the 18th century Enlightenment, had rejected the idea of humanity being fallen and therefore 'sin' had become a taboo word. Though the Christian Gospel is good news, it does begin with the fact that there is a sickness that human beings have which they are born into. According to the Christian view, in the beginning, our ancestors broke a covenant with The Creator, bringing death and sin into the world. Yet The Creator did not abandon his children and creation. He did something that no one could have guessed or expected — He came to this earth as one of us in the first century, suffered a horrible death, and then bodily rose, starting the Christian movement. In order to recover this sense of guilt, Lewis argued in the first few chapters of *Mere Christianity* that there exists a transcendent moral law which cuts across time and culture, and that we have been disobeying this law. If this law does not exist, then morality is completely subjective, a human fabrication, and therefore 'anything goes'.

From there, Lewis's argument leads up to one of the most poignant chapters in *Mere Christianity* in which Lewis asserts that Jesus is the same Jesus of faith and history, claiming to forgive sins, and that He took upon Himself the sins of the world. In conveying this, Lewis critiqued the common idea that Jesus of Nazareth was a 'good moral teacher' that lived in the first century by arguing that Jesus was either God, or a lunatic.

This argument by Lewis is open to criticism, and has often been attacked by thinkers such as Richard Dawkins and Christopher Hitchens. Yet these writers claim that perhaps Jesus of Nazareth never existed. In an interview about his book *God Is Not Great: How Religion Poisons Everything*, atheist Christopher Hitchens said, 'We have no proof, as with Jesus, that he ever existed.' *(https://www.pdxmonthly.com/articles/ 2009/12/17/christopher-hitchens)*

However, this kind of pseudo-historical claim is not taken seriously because of the overwhelming evidence of Jesus's existence. There were Jewish, Pagan, and Roman historians that wrote about Jesus outside of The Bible testifying to his teachings, healings, and how He died for living out what he believed to be his vocation as the Messiah. The messianic movements before Him and after Him that tried to cleanse the temple and overthrow the Romans failed miserably. This messianic movement of Jesus was quite different. His was a movement showing what the Agape love of God was like.

However, out of the movement that Jesus of Nazareth started would come so many different kinds of Christian denominations. This had deeply troubled C. S. Lewis. He knew that this was a great barrier to people experiencing the Agape love of Christ that Christians professed to believe in, and, in order to get past this, Lewis rejected trying to claim that any one particular denomination within the faith was the correct one, and that therefore all the others were false distortions of the Gospel. Though Lewis was a very devout lay Anglican of the Church of England, he expounded in his writings what is known as 'Mere Christianity.' What Lewis meant by this was that there was a unifying factor within Christendom that is found in the Nicene Creed. This creed was written, out of love, by the church fathers to guard against heresies like universalism or Arianism, and to establish what it means to actually be a Christian.

One of the most poignant chapters from *Mere Christianity* is the one called Charity. Charity is not simply being kind, or doing something for someone hoping to get something in return, which would be bargaining and not love at all — Charity, in the Christian sense, is an individual showing the love of Christ by helping the poor, loving your enemy, going the extra mile, and through your vocation, loving and serving people that come across your path. The reason why Lewis could authentically write a chapter like this in a very important theological book is because he displayed charity in his life in numerous ways. Lewis did this because he understood just how broken a sinner he was, and just how much he was in need of grace. One example of Lewis showing charity in his life was during the Second World War when London was being bombed, and evacuee children were sent to go and live with him at his home, The Kilns. Along with this, another great example of charity from Lewis's life is that he gave the money he made from his books to help widows and orphans that desperately needed it.

In 1952 Lewis's BBC radio broadcasts were published as *Mere Christianity*. One of the most important chapters from that book is the chapter on the theological virtue of hope. Lewis critiques the claim that faith is wishful thinking by arguing that there is a transcendent moral law given by God that he calls the Tao in his philosophical work *The Abolition of Man* (p32). He defines a spiritual universal longing for transcendent joy by stating:

If I find in myself a desire which no experience in this world can satisfy, the most probable explanation is that I was made for another world (p136-137).

This experience is bittersweet. As a person consciously living in time and space, I yearn for Heaven and to be in the presence of Christ. Yet, while I am here, I yearn to live a meaningful life by making the most of the here and now.

The German theologian Rudolf Otto called this yearning and longing 'the numinous.' In *The Problem of Pain*, Lewis used this as an argument for the existence of God. This numinous, or mystical experience of transcendent joy, raises many important questions. Why did primitive people have so many gods? Why do human beings long for an eternal paradise? Where does love from? Why did music, literature, painting and other art mediums arise in response to the beauty, terror, pain, suffering, joy and mystery of being alive?

Thinkers like Bertrand Russell, David Hume, and Richard Dawkins argue that all spiritual worldviews are a human fabrication invented because we are horrified of death. The views of these thinkers and the spiritual view of Lewis cannot be both right. (*Miracles* p161-162). In his writings, and in his life, Lewis took on the naturalistic view of the world and argued that the spiritual one was true. An intellectual like himself who had been an atheist for so long could not, in intellectual, emotional and spiritual integrity, reject the mystical experiences of joy he had had as merely biological. These experiences pointed to something outside of himself that was much larger than feeble human reasoning and philosophical propositions. Commenting on the limits of human philosophical understanding, and the reality of a Creator that is far more wise than we, Lewis says that the mystery of prayer can never be proved or disproved in an empirical way. (*The World's Last Night And Other Essays* p6).

But in *Mere Christianity* we have the best example of Lewis's ability to reach a wide audience with the truths that he had personally learned.

George MacDonald: An Anthology

Lewis's *George MacDonald: An Anthology* was published in 1946.

Lewis published this because he owed such a great debt to the Scottish Christian writer, preacher, and mystic, and he wanted, through his influence, to get other people to read MacDonald and experience the Agape Love of God as he did in his own life by reading MacDonald's books.

As a way of showing a great debt to MacDonald, Lewis also wrote him as a character in his book *The Great Divorce*. It is quite a profound expression of gratitude when a writer writes their favorite writer as a character into their own book. That book is a fascinating work about decisions we make in the here and now, in the context of eternity. When the narrator is asking MacDonald's character about heaven and hell, MacDonald replies by saying that in the end, people either choose their own final end, or the presence of God. (p75).

Lewis discovered the writings of MacDonald apparently by accident, but arguably this was one of the ways that The Creator began to work in Lewis's life. After discovering MacDonald, Lewis found that reading him gave him great spiritual nourishment, even though he still considered himself an atheist. Lewis spent hours upon hours reading MacDonald and finding himself more drawn to the person of Christ.

How did George MacDonald come to have such a profound understanding of the Fatherhood of The Creator which would influence the Lewis's view of God's fatherhood? To answer that question, it is important to understand the historical, cultural, and theological context of MacDonald's life.

MacDonald was born in Huntly in 1824, and grew up within a very legalistic Calvinist culture which taught that before an individual was born, he or she was predestined to go to heaven or to hell. MacDonald would eventually become the pastor of a church in Arundel because he sincerely believed that it was his calling. This was not to last for long, though, because MacDonald rejected the 'either/or' approach of Calvinism and Arminianism, and instead believed that many would be reconciled to Christ in the afterlife, that animals may have souls, and that the Bible was inspired but not completely inerrant. These kinds of views went completely against the norm of MacDonald's day, and he was viewed as a heretic.

How did MacDonald respond? He did what Christ commanded all Christians to do — he loved his enemies. In his novels, sermons, poetry, fairy tales, and fantasy works, MacDonald wrote about a just and loving God that cared for all of humanity rather than just a select few, and who was bigger than the systematic theology of John Calvin, Jonathan Edwards, and John Knox. MacDonald questioned the theological assumptions of God's character that these theologians propagated with their view of predestination and election. This Presbyterian reformed theology profoundly impacted the culture of Scotland in MacDonald's time.

One example of the legalistic nature of this culture was when George MacDonald's grandmother burnt a fiddle of his because she believed it to be a satanic snare. Today that would be viewed as absolutely lunacy, but at that time it was a normal thing. My, how times have changed!

It would have been very easy for MacDonald to have simply rejected Christianity altogether, but he did not. He certainly critiqued the fundamentalism of his day, yet he loved those individuals whom he believed were confined to just one particular theological view that prevented them from fully being human.

A highly significant literary experience of Lewis's life that would plant an important seed of *agape* love was when he encountered the theology of George MacDonald through a work of fantasy. When Lewis was a young atheist, he happened to come across a book called *Phantastes*, by George MacDonald, at Leatherhead train station in Surrey, England. Reading it was a powerful experience of transcendent Grace.

It is amazing how, through an obscure Scottish fantasy writer's book, God began to work in Lewis's life — the God he once thought was an imaginary omnipotent fiend! His conversion was not instant of course, and it took him many years to finally come to know the source of the joy that he had experienced through the landscapes of Ireland and England, his personal friendships, Norse and Celtic mythology, and the power and beauty of language as we have seen. But that seemingly small decision he made to purchase a book when he was a young man changed his life, and the lives of many others around the world.

I look back on how a decision I made to go to a small-town county fair has changed my life in a profound way. I remember hearing a song called *Meant to Live,* by a rock band from San Diego, California named Switchfoot. It profoundly moved me. I began to listen to their music, and through it I discovered the writings of Lewis, which made all the difference in my conversion from agnosticism to Christianity. Reading Lewis's fiction, essays, letters, and theological and spiritual works gave me a burning passion for the power of literature and other artistic mediums, helped me to find my voice as a writer, and led me to the writings of MacDonald, including fantasy works such as *Phantastes, Lilith,* and *At the*

Back of the North Wind. His poetry and *Unspoken Sermons* also greatly influenced my faith. I came to understand why he was Lewis's literary hero, and he came to be one of my literary heroes as well.

MacDonald was married to his wife, Louisa, for over fifty years, and, as outlined, had nothing but love for the individuals who attacked him for his theological beliefs. He rejected the legalistic Calvinism of his day, and was a great scholar and writer, and a Scotsman who was proud of his heritage. MacDonald inspires me to live out who I am as Justin Wiggins in Christ, love people of all worldviews, pursue my passion for literature and art, and strive to be gentle, kind, jovial, strong, intelligent, and authentic. It is an honor to be able to honor MacDonald's literary legacy!

Lewis did this in his lifetime by recommending many of MacDonald's books in letters to people who were curious to read him. Without MacDonald's influence, I don't believe Lewis would have been as brilliant as he was, and neither would he have had such a great understanding of the justice, mercy, love, and goodness of God. Though it is quite frustrating that MacDonald is not as well-known as he should be, it does bring me joy to know that there is a community around the world that appreciates his works, just as Lewis did. Lewis made this bold statement about his debt to MacDonald which I have re-read and pondered on quite a lot:

I know hardly any other writer who seems to be closer, or more continually close, to the Spirit of Christ Himself. (George MacDonald An Anthology xxxiv, xxxv).

It could be argued that no other writer had such an impact on C. S. Lewis as George MacDonald.

A Grief Observed

The last book by Lewis in which I shall be examining the theme of *agape* love is *A Grief Observed*.

Among the people that wrote letters to Lewis, one in particular stood out to him and his brother Warren Lewis. It was written by a Jewish American atheist and communist named Joy Davidman Gresham. Joy's Jewish ancestors came from Poland, and they eventually settled in New York. By this time in her life, Joy had been published, was the mother of two boys, and was in a tumultuous marriage with Bill Gresham.

Lewis would have no idea how he would literally be surprised by this brilliant person named Joy in the years to come, and how drastically both their lives life would change. Later, Joy would become a Christian, divorce Bill Gresham, and would move to live in England with her two boys David and Douglas. It took Lewis sometime to catch on to just how much Joy loved him, and it would take her getting deathly sick for Lewis to realize the romantic love that was there which reflected the Agape Love of God. Joy collapsed one day, was rushed to the hospital, and it was revealed that she had bone cancer. Lewis desired to marry her before God, and so an Anglican priest friend of his named Peter Bide officiated the marriage, and laid his hands on Joy asking God to heal her. Miraculously, Joy went into remission for a few years, and they were the happiest years of her and Lewis's life.

These two great writers, human beings and followers of Jesus both had a similar journey in how they were surprised by the Agape love of God through nature, music, literature, and especially the works of MacDonald. In his book *Yet One More Spring: A Critical Study of Joy Davidman*, Lewis scholar Dr. Don King describes their similar experiences of transcendent joy:

The love of fairyland entrenched in Davidman's mind because her early reading of MacDonald prepared the way later for her to cross her atheistic frontier and move to faith in Christ. Lewis's great affection for and debt to MacDonald is well-documented, including the appreciative introduction he wrote for George MacDonald: An Anthology (p220).

With the great love that blossomed between Lewis and Joy Davidman there also came great loss which is the reality of living in a fallen world. Though Joy's cancer had gone into remission, it sadly came back, and she died: Lewis, his brother Warren, and Joy's two sons David and Douglas Gresham all grieved her loss. During this season in Lewis's life, he sincerely questioned whether the Agape Love of God was everlasting and good. After his conversion he had written so prolifically and poignantly about Christianity through fantasy, children's books, essays, theological and spiritual work, poems, and literary criticism. Now, he was going through great grief because he had lost the woman he loved to bone cancer, just as he had lost his mother and father to cancer. He cries out in *A Grief Observed:* 'Cancer, cancer and cancer. My mother, my father, my wife. I wonder who is next in the queue' (p12). His prayers at this time must have been full of panic, anxiety, sorry, anger, and petition.

During this time of bereavement, Lewis began writing a journal about his tumultuous experience with grief. *A Grief Observed* was published in 1961 under the pseudonym of N. W. Clerk since Lewis wanted the book to remain anonymous (p xxvii).

A Grief Observed is an honest, raw book that explores grief, raises questions about how to reconcile the goodness of God and suffering in the world, and outlines how Lewis came to a place where he could finally heal. The most important thing about this book, in my opinion, is how it shows how Lewis's faith was sustained by the Agape Love of God. This was Lewis's most personal and painful experience of the problem of pain. In the first few pages of the book, Lewis poses some very real questions to himself about the goodness of God by asking where is He?

After posing these painful questions, in the end Lewis comes to realize that suffering and loss is part of the love experience in this life, and he finds that his faith in the Agape love of God is strengthened. It would have been so easy for Lewis to reject what he held to be true. He had had a philosophical education, was an atheist for so many years, and had an incredible understanding of language, literature, and different worldview claims. It is quite amazing to me that Lewis's faith was strengthened.

This Irish literary scholar, lay theologian, and Christian apologist knew why he believed what he believed, could match anyone in debate, was jovial, brilliant, humble, truly lived out his faith, wrote some incredible works of literature that have impacted many lives around the world, and he left behind a legacy that is still celebrated today. Lewis was surprised by the Agape love of Christ, and because of that he found his identity, vocation, and was able to communicate that *agape* love to many individuals around the world searching for meaning in their lives.

The Power and Universality
of Art

'C. S. Lewis says that fiction is able to sneak past the watchful dragons of religion,' says Jon Foreman in Switchfoot's *Fading West* film. The documentary explores how the San Diego rockers balance surfing, music, family life, how they live out their faith, and rich traveling adventures to New Zealand, South Africa, Australia, Indonesia, and back to their home in California.

That particular scene where Jon Foreman paraphrases C. S. Lewis is my favorite from the film, and is an important reminder to me of how powerful and universal music, literature, painting, and film are. Someone reads a book by Scottish fantasy writer George MacDonald, and their life is changed; a young, poor mother goes through a horrific bout of depression, and writes an iconic fantasy story called *Harry Potter and the Philosopher's Stone* that helps many people fall in love with reading and changes many lives; a young woman who is suicidal inspires a whole movement called To Write Love on Her Arms because a friend tells her story. This movement comes to help many people who struggle with anxiety, depression, trauma and suicide. These are all examples of how healing and community happen through art. The barriers of politics, religion, and social status come down when people respond to a work of art in the context of their own experience. In my life, music and literature have opened up a whole new world to me, and roused this spiritual hunger that led me to the person of Christ. This universal spiritual hunger C. S. Lewis called 'Joy.'

In his fascinating autobiography *Surprised by Joy*, Lewis records a poignant experience of joy he had as a young boy when he read a poem by Henry Wadsworth Longfellow about the Norse god of beauty and light named Balder (p18-19). Although Lewis asked important theological, historical, and existential questions that were very important in his life, it was this mystical experience of joy that in the end led him to the person of Christ. (*C. S. Lewis On Joy* Lesley Walmsley p 6). In his book *The Oxford Inklings*, scholar Colin Duriez writes:

This was an inconsolable longing or 'Sweet Desire' that nothing in human experience, whether of nature or art or human love, could satisfy. He slowly discovered that its fulfillment lay beyond the world, in God himself. By centering on Joy, Lewis found an affinity with the 'Romantic' tradition of Wordsworth, Coleridge, George MacDonald, and many others who wrote long before the Romantic Movement, such as the poets of Henry Vaughan and Thomas Traherne (p 107).

It is absolutely fascinating that an intellectual such as Lewis did not dismiss this mystical joy as something that was simply a delusion which could not be taken seriously. Instead, it became the most important thing in his life. This desire led him outside of himself, his books, and burning ambition to be a great poet. In the end, Lewis found that this desire had really no value in itself, except to lead him to the person of Jesus Christ.

When this happened, scores of books flowed from his pen, and volumes of letters began to pour in. Lewis felt it was his duty to answer every letter that was written to him because he felt responsible to his readers in the context of his vocation as a writer lay theologian evangelist. (*Yours, Jack* p V). In his biography on Lewis, author Terry Glaspey writes this regarding the romantic joy experienced in his childhood that would eventually lead him to God:

At the time, this was the closest thing to a religious experience he was to have, since the family religion of his childhood meant little to him. This experience, similar to that described by William Wordsworth and Thomas Traherne, was, in reality a desire for, and a sense of, the presence of God. (Not A Tame Lion p 29).

Lewis was able to be of great help to many people, and to offer great counsel to those who were struggling with different issues. Clyde S. Kilby, who compiled *A Mind Awake: An Anthology of C. S. Lewis*, gives a great example of how Lewis helped people out of his service to God:

By his own admission awkward in his social affairs, he acted on his conviction of Christian duty to sit at the bedside of the sick and personally serve the poor. He gave away two-thirds of his income... (Kilby p X).

It is absolutely amazing that this mystical experience of joy led Lewis to embracing a worldview that made him forget about himself, allowed him to help many people around the world through his writings, and made him (there is some irony here) one of the world's most popular Christian writers.

In his book *C. S. Lewis A Biography of Friendship*, Colin Duriez writes very poignantly about Lewis's understanding of myth, history, and Christianity:

The Gospels accounts were (as he learned through Tolkien) the highest point of human storytelling and myth-making, with an astounding dimension of historical veracity. Everything was true in the actual, primary world, without losing the quality of myth that engendered Joy. (p 133).

Christianity was no longer something associated with childhood, the primitive past, or wish fulfillment. Christianity became the worldview that Lewis found meaning in, that he defended as an apologist, and that was something he lived out. Lewis would have no idea how much of an impact he would have as a writer and lay theologian. The way he brought together imagination, reason, faith, and personal experience was unique.

Before Lewis's conversion, he wrote two important works of poetry, *Spirits in Bondage* and *Dymer*. Both of these poetic works capture the contradiction that Lewis had in his life of his spiritual experiences stirred by beauty, and his atheism which, as mentioned, only hardened after he was tutored by the brilliant William Kirkpatrick, whom he referred to as 'The Great Knock' in *Surprised by Joy*. The two volumes of poetry did not receive the public attention that Lewis was hoping for. Yet, later in his life, some of Lewis's poems would be published, and his understanding of poetry as a literary scholar was considered absolutely brilliant (*Image and Imagination* p 99).

Though Lewis loved debate and was a brilliant thinker who could match anyone that engaged in a philosophical dialogue with him, it was not a historical, theological, or philosophical argument that brought him to faith. It was this deep longing he called 'Joy' he experienced in the landscape of Ireland and England, when reading the Norse and Celtic myths, the music of Wagner, the works of his literary hero George MacDonald, George Herbert, William Butler Yeats, and Beatrix Potter. Lewis could not just explain this mystical experience away by simply saying that it was only an emotional reaction going on in the brain. Even the naturalism of Sigmund Freud, and philosophical arguments from the first anti-theistic thinkers like Epicurus did not convince him that naturalism was true. This deep yearning, called *sehnsucht* in German, could not be explained away by scientific empiricism as something that is only natural.

The German word *sehnsucht* is defined as a longing that no amount of sex, love, money, or earthly happiness can satisfy. This aching desire, that is a combination of grief and joy, is what led the young atheist Lewis from theism, to Christianity, and is what brought me from agnosticism to the person of Christ years ago. After his conversion, Lewis connected this yearning with his desire for Heaven, and the desire to know The Creator. Perhaps we are not just stardust, chemicals and atoms; perhaps we were made for a world that we are exiled from?

Four further works by Lewis tell how *sehnsucht* led him to the person of Christ — *Surprised by Joy, The Weight of Glory, Perelandra,* and *Till We Have Faces.* I will now briefly examine them.

Surprised by Joy

Since humanity's beginning, there has always been spiritual experience.

Different cultures have had shrines, temples, male and female spiritual leaders, people have buried their dead with treasure, food, celebrated special holy days about death and new life, had different deities of the sun, moon, winter, stars, sea, sky, war, sex, and love, architecture, music, poetry and things written down in holy books. Though these cultures may be different, the one common thing about them is that they are all expressing a yearning and longing for something outside of themselves. One could argue that this religious experience is a human delusion that is simply a cultural fabrication invented by human beings because of fear rather than it pointing to something outside of time and space that was not invented by human beings. You could also argue that because there are so many different expressions of spirituality and similarities between different religions, that it is a very real universal experience to humanity (*The Discarded Image* p 1).

One iconic writer that found himself facing these two conflicting worldviews was the Irish lay theologian and literary scholar C. S. Lewis. As we have seen, Lewis connected this experience of joy to something outside of himself that transcended time and culture, and that led him to embracing the Christian faith. When he wrote and published his autobiography in 1955, Lewis chose to call it *Surprised by Joy*. The title comes from a William Wordsworth poem, and in this autobiography, he tried to capture how he made the leaps from atheism to theism, and then to Christianity through the spiritual experiences he called 'joy'. The first part of the book begins with Lewis describing a few important experiences of this joy he had had in his life, growing up in Belfast, Northern Ireland.

As outlined earlier, Lewis grew up within a Christian worldview in the North of Ireland. Growing up, Lewis experienced quite a lot of tragedy with the loss of his mother and experiencing the hell of the First World War. As we have seen, this, combined with the influence of his atheist tutor William Kirkpatrick, his discovery of Norse and Celtic mythology, and the different philosophers he read, brought Lewis to the conclusion that all religions were human inventions. Yet the spiritual experiences that he had through works of literature, nature, music, and the important relationships in his life would completely contradict his philosophy of life. For many years, Lewis resisted the fact that perhaps this spiritual experience he called joy pointed to something outside of himself. As we have been reading, he eventually he became a theist in 1929, and a Christian in 1931.

What, according to Lewis himself, had played a huge role in this and how did this happen?

To Lewis, myth was not just interesting primitive stories that were obviously false, but actually contained truth that came to be fulfilled in Christianity, but he did not come to fully understand this until his friend, philologist, and author of *The Hobbit* and *The Lord of the Rings*, J. R. R. Tolkien, pointed out to him that his view of myth was distorted by his erroneous naturalistic assumptions. This unsettled him, and on a late night at Addison's walk in 1931 with Hugo Dyson and Tolkien, he came to understand that the old story of the dying and rising god of Balder, Osiris, and Adonis, came true in the Incarnation, Death, and Resurrection of Jesus in first century Palestine. Lewis finally came to understand how this yearning led him to something outside of himself. Everything that roused this longing brought him to the person of Jesus Christ.

Now C. S. Lewis had something to say as a writer, and in his writings, he set out to communicate why this joy was so important as a universal human experience, and why he believed that it was fulfilled within Christianity. While he did this poignantly in works like *Mere Christianity,* and other works, as we have seen, in my opinion, he did this best in his fiction.

Through myth, Lewis was able to communicate Christian truths in a way that people of different worldviews could relate to, and that would not be such a barrier because of those different theological views. By doing this, Lewis was able to communicate Christianity to people who loathed organized religion or who perhaps had had a bad experience with brain washing or proselytizing.

Jesus of Nazareth told stories in the first century to communicate things to people about justice, faith, hope, and love to anyone that was willing to come to Him. Lewis followed this model of his Lord and Savior, and has had a profound impact on culture and many people's lives. He was a master storyteller and apologist, but he knew that it was all God's grace that was working through him.

Perelandra

Lewis sought to translate his experience of *sehn*sucht in the second book in his cosmic trilogy called *Perelandra*. The character Ransom, the philologist, is the protagonist, and is based on Lewis's friend J. R. R. Tolkien who was a philologist.

This fascinating novel is his retelling of the ancient Genesis story, set on the planet Venus. In the story Ransom is chosen by Oyarsa, the god of Malacandra, to do battle against the forces of evil on a newly created planet. Ransom is overwhelmed by the beauty of this Edenic paradise — perhaps the experience of joy that Lewis had as a young child when he was with his brother Warren, as well as the landscapes of Ireland and England that he dearly loved, inspired him to write so many passages of beautiful prose in this book. The landscape of *Perelandra* stirs a poignant longing in Ransom. Lewis describes it:

It was sharp, sweet, wild, and holy all in one, and in any world where men's nerves have ceased to obey their central desires would doubtless have been aphrodisiac too, but not in Perelandra. (p 88)

I would argue that this is one of the powerful passages in any book by Lewis. Here, he describes this fictional character's response to beauty in a newly created world that is perfect. This is something that we in our fallen world have lost because of our ancestors' rebellion against The Creator. We all long for our true home, which is not in this world, but we have glimpses in this life which stir this ache — we are homesick for home. To Lewis, this was not escapism, but a very important reminder that though our home is in heaven, we are to live in the here and now in the context of eternity. Faith in an afterlife often gets branded as something that is wishful thinking, and there have of course been terrible things done in the name of religion. However, any worldview can be abused, and therefore a caricature can be given of a particular religion.

Ransom eventually meets the Green Lady who is the ruler of the planet, just as Eve is the first woman that is written about in the creation story found in Genesis. Ransom finds himself amazed at her beauty, and that she does not know good nor evil as he does since she is not a fallen human being. The theme of myth comes into the novel when Ransom reflects on what is actually happening on *Perelandra* when he is in the presence of the Green Lady, and they go looking for the King.

In our post-modern world, myth is something that is often viewed as false and therefore irrelevant. Why would we go back to primitive superstition in our progressive world? Aren't myths just false stories that are not true? Lewis rejected this view of myth. He viewed myth as a revelation from God rather than something which is no longer relevant to modern day life. The ancient pagan myths, to Lewis, were fulfilled in Christianity, and the Greek, Norse, and Celtic myths had roused the joy that had led him to faith.

At the end of *Perelandra* after the planet is saved and the King and Queen are re-united, Lewis describes the new paradise in mythical language. He incorporates his love for myth, brilliance as a scholar of medieval and renaissance literature, and his desire for the new heavens and the new earth. We can only speculate as to what it will be like when we are at home in the presence of Christ. The ending of Lewis's novel is him attempting to describe that anticipated joy. Of all of Lewis's fiction, *Perelandra* is my favorite by him. His description of the landscapes, philosophical debates between Ransom, Weston, and the Green Lady, the transcendent joy that he describes Ransom experiencing, and the end of the book when the planet is saved and the King and Queen are re-united in love, is all quite a profound literary experience for the reader.

The Weight of Glory

In 1941, during the Second World War, at St. Mary The Virgin church in Oxford, Lewis preached one of his most famous and quoted essays, *The Weight of Glory.* In his sermon, Lewis critiques the materialistic view of spiritual longing by arguing that there is no empirical evidence for this view, and that the joy we experience through nature, books, music, and beauty, is a universal human experience that points beyond ourselves to a Creator, and to heaven, which is our true home. If this is not true, then joy is simply a chemical reaction going on in the brain, and all ends in death. However, if this longing is a universal real experience, then death is not the end, and eternity makes the here and now meaningful. (p 29-31).

Lewis realized that it would have been idolatry to worship the Norse and Celtic gods, the music of Wagner, and the writings that roused the joy in his life he was always searching for. He also recognized that works of art arouse joy and reflect the glory and beauty of God, just as human beings do, since we are all living works of art.

The Weight of Glory & Ireland

What a day that must have been in 1941! In Oxford, England, a packed crowd of people that were inquisitive, and hungry for hope and meaning came to see the great Irish writer, C. S. Lewis, preach a sermon that is one of his most powerful pieces of writing that was compiled in a book called *The Weight of Glory and other Addresses* in 1941. I remember sitting inside St. Marty The Virgin Church and reading *The Weight of Glory* numerous times. I love the fact that in the sermon Lewis conveys, with great humility and conviction, that the source of all beauty, goodness, and truth, is The Great Artist, Christ. It was the beauty roused by music, books, and film which helped convince me that spiritual experience is not a delusion that can be explained away by scientific empiricism, but a reality experienced by millions around the world. The iconic sermon by Lewis is worth reading numerous times, and one always find some important reminder in it about the hope and joy found in Christ in the context of the brevity of life.

The sad loss of his mother during his childhood in Belfast Northern, Ireland, was quite a heavy blow, and certainly made the young Irishman aware of the brevity of life. It was a great loss that Lewis never fully recovered from, but, in his life, he found that he was able to cope with the loss because of the Agape love of Christ.

The island of his birth, Ireland, was always dear to Lewis's heart. Although most people think of him as an English Oxford tutor and lay theologian, he was always an Irishman at heart. In many places in his fiction, letters, poetry, and non-fiction, Lewis conveyed his great love for Ireland. I find it incredibly moving, that he took his wife Joy Davidman on a honeymoon to Ireland — the island of his birth. Lewis had a glimpse of Tír na nÓg in his life, and did a very brilliant job, in his daily life, and writings, to convey that eternal longing every person has for their Creator — The Great Artist Christ.

Till We Have Faces

Ever since Lewis had been a young teenager he had been haunted by the Greek myth of Cupid and Psyche.

At a time in his life when he had a burning ambition to become a great poet, he wrote his own poetic versions of this myth. Later in his literary career, he wanted to try his hand at this myth which had haunted him from his youth, but lamented that he felt his creative ability as a writer was beginning to dwindle. One day he expressed this to his wife Joy Davidman at their home The Kilns in Headington a few miles outside of Oxford, and she encouraged him to try his hand at this story.

As soon as Lewis began writing the first chapter, it began to flow from his pen like a North Carolina mountain stream. Lewis dedicated *Till We Have Faces* to his wife, and it was published in 1956. Lewis said he thought it was his best work, though it did not get the public attention that his Narnia stories and popular theological works did.

In the story, Psyche, who is the sister of Orual, falls in love with the god of the mountain, who is Cupid. When this happens, Orual feels betrayed and thinks that Psyche is deluded. In the character of Psyche, Lewis writes poignantly about the transcendent joy which was the most powerful thing in his life:

The sweetest thing in all my life has been the longing — to reach the Mountain, to find the place where all the beauty came from — my country, the place where I ought to have been born. Do you think it all meant nothing, all the longing? The longing for home? For indeed it now feels not like going, but like going back.

In the dialogue between Orual and Psyche, one can see how central joy was to Lewis's life, and why he viewed beauty as something which pointed to a world beyond ours. In the end of *Till We Have Faces*, Orual comes to finally understand that Psyche was not deluded, that her yearning and longing was to be united with the god of love, Cupid, and that she was tyrannically selfish of her sister. It is a very unique work by Lewis, and one of its most important themes is the joy which was central to his life. I find it charming that Lewis dedicated this book to his wife Joy, who actually helped him edit it. Years after he would sadly lose Joy to bone cancer, Lewis said of her personality:

Her mind was lithe and quick and muscular as a leopard. Passion, tenderness, and pain were all equally unable to disarm it. (A Grief Observed p 4-5).

In Lewis's essay, *Myth Became Fact*, published in 1944, he argues that myth is not irrational, embarrassing, or diabolical, but something through which God has revealed Himself to humanity in different times and places. As we have seen, this yearning and longing is essential to understanding Lewis, because it led him from atheism, theism to the person of Christ, and is something that is universal to human experience. Inkling scholar Colin Duriez said:

Lewis's technical name for this longing (the Sehnsucht of German Romanticism) was Joy, a 'sweet desire' that no human experience of love, beauty, art, or literature could satisfy. It was to become a major theme in his writings. (p 67).

C. S. Lewis
and the Importance of Books

It was not until I was around the age of 19 that I discovered a great zeal and passion for books, whereas before, I was abysmally ignorant of why art and books are important to our human tribe, and thought they were simply a form of escapism that had nothing to do with real life — the kind of culture in which I grew up viewed them in quite a derogatory, utilitarian way. I read a few books growing up here and there, and did enjoy spending a lazy afternoon or evening immersed in a book, but for the most part it was compulsory reading I had to do for school in order to get a grade so I wouldn't flunk. Things turned out quite interesting when through an American musician and an Irish writer my entire way of seeing the world was transformed. I became fascinated with the origin of language and art, myths, legends, and how language started with primitive cave paintings, oral storytelling tradition, and then on to the hardback and paperback book. When I discovered that great love for books, it was great to find people who also shared that same love for books and spoke my language — it would be like growing up with Irish Gaelic as your native tongue and finding people in the United States who spoke it after moving there from your native country of Ireland not knowing anyone. Two particular modern books called *The Guernsey Literary Potato Pie Peel Society* by Anne Morrow, and *84 Charing Cross Road* by Helene Hanff, are two fascinating works of literature that are great odes to books. *Guernsey* is a work of historical fiction set in during World War II on the Isle of Guernsey that explores a community of people who deal with the trauma of the war by sharing their love for books, and of course there is an engaging love story involved, inspired by the famous Jane Austen. *84 Charing Cross Road* is a series of charming, funny, and moving letters written between an American writer in New York and in London, England all about the great importance of books. These two great books are prominent modern examples of the fact that people still take the time to read, even in our technological age of iPhones, tablets, laptops, and very short attention spans. I can't imagine a world without books, and though I do not have the gift of prophecy, I do hope that they never go out of fashion and are always sustained by the innate human need for narrative. Whenever I am a work, or at a coffee shop, or a public place and see people actually with a book in their hands, I always smile and am filled with hope. Working at Books A Million in New Bern, North Carolina, and Barnes and Noble in Asheville, NC, gave me an even greater zeal for books and the narrative called life being written by the Great Artist.

Three particular memories stand out to me from Barnes and Noble. The first was talking to an English lady when I was working a shift in the café. I noticed her accent, I asked her where she was from, and the subject of books came up. She told me she and a book club of hers were reading *The*

Lion, the Witch, and the Wardrobe by C. S. Lewis. She shared with me memories of her reading it during childhood, and I was reminded of the wonder it filled me with when I read it for the first time. I love the soundtrack from the film as well. The second memory was when I was working a shift as a bookseller one day, and met this kind Irish lady as I was making sure the fantasy and science fiction section was aesthetically pleasing to the eyes of people browsing around. After talking a bit with the lady, my eyes got quite big and my jaw dropped when she told me that she had met J. R. R. Tolkien himself when she was a young lass. That was an amazing moment.

The third experience I had was during the busy holiday season I struck up a conversation with this kind professor that taught at UNC Asheville. He was telling me about a class he taught on fantasy, C. S. Lewis, J. R. R. Tolkien, Ursula K. Le Guin, and other writers. After I told him something about myself, my book *Surprised by Agape,* and that I was glad to know that he was teaching that particular course, he invited me to give a talk to his class, and I was greatly humbled and thankful he would even bother to ask me. I was quite nervous, but I prepared for the talk, put together some slides on a PowerPoint, showed a few relevant videos, and shared with the students about how I survived suicide, toxic religious fundamentalism, came to embrace what I believe, and how my passion for writing, literature and art became a vocation. It certainly wasn't easy sharing with the students in the room such personal experiences, but I found it helped them open up, and to my great delight, many of them shared with me particular books, songs, video games, and writers that had a profound impact on their lives.

I will always remember that night at UNC Asheville — very different people coming together over a common passion for books. Whether it is poetry, biography, memoir, philosophy, history, religion, science, spirituality, politics, culture, psychology, fiction, or humor, books are great sacramental gifts to the world. They influence your beliefs, move you, challenge you, make you weep, laugh, experience joy, provide engaging and interesting conversations, bring lovers, friends, and community together, and change lives.

Visiting C. S. Lewis's Home
The Kilns

For years I had been wanting the opportunity to visit the home of my favorite writer, C. S. Lewis, and when that finally came to fruition, I felt like the Pevensie children did when they first looked Aslan in his wild and majestic face, or when the ring was destroyed and all of Middle-earth was saved. I still remember quite vividly riding there in a van from Oxford, England with students from Montreat College, and my friend Dr. Don King, and his wife Jeanne King, and when we arrived at the house in Headington, I was filled with *sehnsucht*— I was at the threshold where Narnia was written! The Narnia books have meant so much to millions of people around the world, and continue to be Jack Lewis's bestselling books, because although they were written by a twentieth century Irish Christian scholar and lay theologian, these stories about peril, human depravity, the depths of agape love, magic, adventure, and courage, are universal to the human experience. Recently I finished re-reading *The Chronicles of Narnia* again. I remember the very night, years ago, I purchased the one-volume set at the Barnes and Noble in Greenville, North Carolina. At that time in my life, I was an agnostic and yearning for meaning; and it was the way Lewis wrote about Christianity in the form of fairy tales that allowed me to see it in a whole new light — the faith was no longer associated with psychological manipulation, cultural fundamentalism, pious arrogance, political propaganda, and denominational feuds. I finally understood the faith as it was historically in the first century by reading these stories, had a gradual conversion, came to know Christ, found a passion for writing, music, literature, and art, read anything by Lewis I could get my hands on; came to have an amazing community, rich experiences I marvel at; came to appreciate people of different worldviews, and discovered many other writers.

The day we had a tour of the charming home in the village of Headington, which is a few miles outside of Oxford, was a chilly and lovely March day under a blue English sky. As we walked from room to room, and our tour guide Nicole described what daily life was like for Lewis, his brother Warnie, Mrs. Moore, Joy Davidman, and David and Doug Gresham, it was all quite moving to hear about. So much rich literary history happened in that home — there Lewis wrote some of the Narnia books, *The Screwtape Letters*, *The Allegory of Love*, *The Great Divorce*, *Till We Have Faces*, and many other iconic works. While I was there, I imagined to myself the joy that must have beamed from Lewis's face when he was writing so many of the works that we all greatly admire. There also must have been looks of exhaustion on his face when he replied to every single letter that was written to him, and he would spend hours every day responding, which speaks volumes about his character. Along with the home tour, there was also the lovely nature reserve, which certainly reminded me of Kenneth Grahame's *The Wind in The Willows*. My favorite part of the trip was seeing the desk where Lewis would have looked out the window, dipped his pen, enjoyed his pipe tobacco, a good cup of tea, and wrote — the Irish writer's prose flows like a North Carolina mountain stream. One of the more sobering experiences which happened when I was at The Kilns was being in the same room where Lewis died in 1963, the same day that American President John F. Kennedy was assassinated, and the writer Aldous Huxley died. I thought about how painful it must have been for Warnie Lewis to find his brother unconscious, and for Doug Gresham to lose his beloved stepfather. No doubt Lewis was welcomed from these shadowlands to the true Narnia, and in the end, he found the source of the *sehnsucht* joy which had haunted him throughout his life. That trip to The Kilns was very special for me, and I look forward to seeing the hallowed place again someday. Let us thank the hardworking volunteers who restored Lewis's home from its appalling condition, and the C. S. Lewis Foundation in Redlands, California, for doing such a fine job of honoring Lewis's literary legacy by taking care of the home — Providence on display no doubt!

The Legacy of
George MacDonald

Scotland is a fascinating and beautiful country that has given the world some of the greatest poets, musicians, and artists, and writers. One of those great writers from the Isle of Alba is the Scottish writer, poet, and mythmaker George MacDonald. MacDonald was descended from a clan that was almost completely slaughtered at the massacre at Glencoe. The place is said to be haunted, and it is a miracle that MacDonald himself came into existence.

MacDonald is sadly not as widely read as C. S. Lewis would have liked him to be, which is one reason why Lewis compiled his *George MacDonald An Anthology* in 1946. The first time I came across the book I was browsing around in a Barnes and Noble and when I read these words, tears came to my eyes:

That man is perfect in faith who can come to God in the utter dearth of his feelings and desires, without a glow or an aspiration, with the weight of low thoughts, failures, neglects, and wandering forgetfulness, and say to Him, 'Thou art my refuge.' (George MacDonald An Anthology, Lewis.)

A line like that comes from a human being who has a profound understanding, by experience and not the intellect

95

alone, that we are all loved by a good and loving Creator. For MacDonald to come to this kind of hopeful view in his life, took a great deal of unlearning a fierce hyper-Calvinism which was deeply ingrained in the Scottish culture he grew up in. Many readers have found solace in MacDonald's theology because they themselves have been deeply wounded by some negative experience with organized religion which involved brainwashing. The God George MacDonald came to believe in was greater than a vindictive Jove or Zeus-like deity that cared only for having its wrath appeased or its beloved glory on display. The God he believed in came for the rescue of all of humanity in the first century through Jesus of Nazareth's incarnation, Death, and Resurrection — agape love on display which is greater than sin, death, and the powers of hell. What mortal can comprehend that great depth of everlasting love?

Here in 2021, many more people are discovering the writings of MacDonald through word of mouth, articles, blogs online, through Inklings' conferences, scholarly papers and books inspired by his theology and literary legacy, and through my Scottish friend David Jack's translations of MacDonald's novels from the Doric into English. David is a very good friend, and has done an amazing job with these new translations through the worksofmacdonald.com website. My most cherished book by MacDonald is a Penguin edition book of his fairy tales that I got from Waterstones in Oxford, England when I was with David. That book brings back that very special memory.

In his life, George MacDonald went through much failure pursuing a career as a preacher, struggled with poverty, suffered quite a lot, but yet was a great Scotsman of faith, a good husband, father, a prolific writer, friends with Mark Twain, Alfred Lord Tennyson, John Ruskin, and left behind quite an amazing literary legacy. I understand more and more why C. S. Lewis praised his writings so much, and I am very glad that many people today are discovering the rich works of George MacDonald. The Scotsman should be as well-known as Sir Walter Scott, Robert Burns, J. M. Barrie, and Robert Louis Stevenson.

One of the most baffling things I ever experienced was once when I met these wonderful people at a favorite local coffee shop, heard their Scottish accents, and we struck up a good conversation about Scotland and different writers. "Have you ever heard of George MacDonald?" I asked with great excitement. They shook their heads with a blank stare and responded with, "No, we haven't." I gladly recommended MacDonald to them. The rest of the conversation was quite pleasant, but I was very perplexed that these kind and charming people from Scotland had never heard of one of the greatest writers that came out of Scotland — it would be like if I had lived in Russia and never heard of Leo Tolstoy or Fyodor Dostoevsky.

The first book that I ever read by George MacDonald was *The Princess and The Goblin*. The particular edition I read was a worn Penguin children's classic that was less than five dollars. As I was reading through it, I imagined George MacDonald writing it with a smile on his face, and then telling this enchanting and captivating tale to his children and wife as they gathered around the fireplace to listen to this story which would eventually become a classic. In the story, Irene's great grandmother is, to some degree, like Aslan in Lewis's Narnia series — she is mysterious, strong, wise, ancient, and wild but also good. After I finished the story I found myself loving Christ more, and became a devoted admirer of MacDonald — I wanted to read everything that the Scotsman wrote, and biographies on him, so I could understand why he was so referred by many writers, though he is still not as well known today as he should be, which is quite baffling.

Many young people in my generation have suffered the appalling reality of being abandoned by a father or mother. This great wound causes difficult and complex issues with depression, trauma, anxiety, and this constant fear of being abandoned even by people who are always there for you. Although George MacDonald sadly lost his mother at a very young age, he was fortunate to have a loving father who was truly there for him. One of the most important aspects of MacDonald's writings is his description of agape love — Cosmo's bond with his father from *Castle Warlock*, Robert being reunited with his father who was a former addict in *Robert Falconer*, and the fairy godmother figure in his fairy tales. In his fascinating scholarly work, *God's Fiction: Symbolism and Allegory in the works of George MacDonald*, Scotsman scholar from the University of Dundee, David Ross, writes movingly of his fellow countryman:

In MacDonald's eyes, true religion and genuine art point in the same direction to God. (ibid.)

That simple line sums up MacDonald's sacramental vision which has changed many people's lives around the world. I praise Christ for the great Scotsman!

J. R. R. Tolkien

I remember years ago browsing around this favorite used bookshop in Greenville, North Carolina, which is now sadly closed, and finding a paperback copy of Humphrey Carpenter's book called *The Inklings* which was first published in 1978. The book had been on my list to read for a while and finding it for quite cheap as a paperback was incredibly exciting.

By that point, I had read only a little of Lewis, Tolkien, Charles Williams, and MacDonald, so Carpenter's book was very enlightening on the dynamic friendship between the Inklings, differences in their personalities, views on literature and myth, different philosophical and theological views, and the bond of friendship and a mutual love for literature and story which kept the group meeting for many years.

Years later, I would have the opportunity to meet scholar and writer Colin Duriez, whose book *The Oxford Inklings: Lewis, Tolkien, and Their Circle* I have read many times. It was great meeting Colin in Montreat, North Carolina, at an Inklings retreat, and talking with him about Celtic Christianity, N. T. Wright, Charles Williams' view of co-inherence, his forthcoming book on Dorothy Sayers which is now out, and the shared admiration we both had of Lewis, Tolkien, and MacDonald's works. It was one of the best conversations of my life, and to my utter joy, years later, I would get to go on an Inklings tour with him and his wife Cindy Zudys on a fine March Day in Oxford. Going with them to Addison's Walk, The Lamb and Flag pub, Magdalen College, Christ Church Meadow, and walking the streets of Oxford, was such a great delight. In conversation with Colin at The Lamb and Flag, I still vividly remember talking with him about the numinous evoked in Tolkien's work, and that gave me the desire to re-read *The Lord of the Rings*, which has become my favorite work of fiction.

It is amazing to me that although J. R. R. Tolkien sadly was an orphan, and lost many of his friends in the hell of World War I, he was still able to function, became an incredible Oxford professor, believed in a good and loving Creator, married his beloved Edith, who was also an orphan, and inspired his Luthien and Arwen characters in his mythology, and gave the world some great works of literature like *The Hobbit*, *The Silmarillion*, and his masterpiece *The Lord of The Rings*.

This man is such an inspiration to me, and his works have made me weep tears of joy; he inspires me to pursue my passion for writing, literature, and art, live out my faith, love people of different worldviews, love with passion, and strive to be gentle, kind, brave, honest, and jovial.

One of the most fascinating aspects from Tolkien's mythology is the race of beings called hobbits. They represent very earthy and rustic people who love beer, coffee, pipe tobacco, the countryside, food, cheer, talk, tea, and sometimes, adventure. For generations, people around the world have been delighted with Bilbo Baggins adventure story of how he is taken out of his comfort zone and comes back a changed hobbit — this theme of exile and returning home certainly correlates to Tolkien's own life, and his mythology.

All of Tolkien's life was a journey to his true home in the presence of Christ, and he never abandoned that hope within him that he was taught by his mother; and though one can read *The Hobbit* and *The Lord of the Rings* simply for the joy of the stories in themselves (which is what Tolkien aimed to do) they are still filled with the faith which gave his life great joy and meaning.

Considering all the great loss and suffering Tolkien endured, I believe it was very brave of him to do what he did in his life with his writing, vocation as a philologist, the love he bore for his wife and family, and the faith in Christ which sustained him. It could have been very easy for Tolkien to reject what he was taught to be true at a young age, but, he defiantly affirmed his belief in a good and loving God, despite deep wounds which no doubt caused him much trauma and struggles with pessimism.

As a joke, my Scottish friend David Jack has called me 'Wiggins of Wig-End' which I take as a compliment, as many friends have also told me that I am very 'hobbit-like.' That compliment is an honor.

C. S. Lewis & Ireland

Once upon a time a young Belfast-born Irish lad sadly loses his Mother, becomes wounded in a terrible war, but through the landscape of his beloved Ireland, and England, through reading the great myths, finding solace in the healing power of music, literature and art, having encouragement from kindred spirts he meets on his journey, and his burning passion for writing, he finds the great treasure of hope on his quest. And once he finds that hope, he becomes a man. Once upon a time a young confused lad grows up in a small peculiar town in North Carolina. He suffers from depression, father abandonment struggles, agonizing philosophical questions, comes close to death numerous times, and yet, through the help of an Irish writer from Belfast, and the healing power of music, literature, and art, he becomes a writer, a man, and finds a home in the primitive, majestic, mountains of North Carolina.

Getting to write about your favorite writer, as well as your favorite country, is a very exciting thing indeed. When I visited Ireland for the first time I felt a deeper connection with the Ulsterman C. S. Lewis. I thought Oxford, England was amazing (and of course it is) but I was not prepared for how life-changing going to Ireland would be. The beautiful County Antrim coast, the Giant's Causeway, Dunluce Castle, and seeing the Mourne Mountains in the distance, inspired three of my books and helped me understand why C. S. Lewis loved Ireland so much. All of that wild Celtic landscape inspired the geography of Narnia, and many of Lewis's other books. Actually seeing it all in person felt like I was on the borders of Faerie, and I am quite sure I was near the realm of Tír na nÓg. I was filled with a profound bittersweet desire to journey to the mystical isle, and perhaps someday I shall find myself there.

My experience in Ireland brought a peculiar question to my mind —how can one feel at home in a country one has never visited? What does that question mean to you? It is a question that led me to Christ, the Great Bard, just as it led Lewis to Christ. The Great Bard drew me to C. S. Lewis's writings, to Ireland, sustained me through hellish pain that almost killed me numerous times, gave me a great passion for writing and art, joy in the present, and a hope for the future, pubs, and bookshops. I love the Risen King with the wounds of agape love on His hands with all my mind, heart, and soul. That is my personal story, and you, dear reader, have your own unique life narrative.

I love how music, literature, and art bring people together of so many different worldviews. I was reminded of that one fine August night at *The Brazen Head* pub in Dublin. All the people in that pub were spellbound as the brilliant Irish musicians were playing — Celtic hospitality at its finest! As much as I love England and Scotland, Ireland is my favorite place that I have ever been to, and will always be so. I worked really hard to get there, found a cheap flight from America, and to my utter joy, I finally got to see places that inspired my favorite writer, C. S. Lewis, and other writers that I am quite fond of, such as John O'Donohue, Seamus Heaney, William Butler Yeats, Oscar Wilde, and James Joyce. These writers were from the land of ancient Celtic myths of old such as Tír na nÓg , the Tuatha Dé Danann, and the Children of Danu; the land of Bards, Druids, great Irish Kings, and Celtic Saints such as Brigid, Hilda, and Patrick.

I got to spend my birthday in 2021 in Dublin, met some very hospitable Irish people, got a lot of inspiration for writing, reveled in the beauty of the landscape and culture, loved Belfast, Cullybackey, Slemish, Lahinch, Bellaghy, the Cliffs of Moher, the Giant's Causeway, the Guinness Factory, Hodges Figgis bookshop, and other places. Thank you C. S. Lewis for giving me a great love for the island of your birth. Below is a poem called *Ode to C. S. Lewis* which conveys my gratitude for the great Irish writer.

Slainte!

Ode to C. S. Lewis

Great Irish writer whose books changed my life!
Through Jon Foreman's music I discovered you,
When I was scared, lonely, depressed, and wanted to die
In that yearning for death, there was a desperate cry,
To know if the ancient dying and rising god story was actually true,
And if so, could this Christ-God heal, restore, and renew,
My weary body, soul, heart, and mind?
An affirmative yes, as I experienced an agape love greater than my
Doubts, questions, and intense pain,

C. S. Lewis experienced this same life changing agape love,
As he sank to his knees in repentance, and found his intellectual snobbery and shame
Dissolved, as he discovered the source of the transcendent joy,
Roused by the Irish myth of Tír na nÓg, Norse Mythology, landscape, and art,
His great void, became fulfilled,
As he set out with a new mind and heart
To pursue his literary vocation!
The way Lewis describes the numinous Aslan singing Narnia into being,
Ransom's mystical experience of being in the presence of Perelandra's King and Queen
His great devotion to his beloved Joy Davidman Lewis,
His humility, charity, friendships, love for myth, and Christ,
I continuously find inspiring
As I seek to dream, love, laugh, work, read, and write!

Conclusion

Every work of Art that deeply moves me reminds me that this life is a story, a quest, not a philosophical system to be figured out. All questions will never be answered. This world is broken and fallen, but it is also a place of great beauty and complexity, and I believe it reflects the glory and beauty of The Creator. How have I experienced life as a living work of Art? Through community, experiences of love, beauty, and joy; pursuing my passion for literature, surviving suicide, embracing who I was created to be as Justin Wiggins, and writing this book.

The Great Artist wove events of my life together into a beautiful tapestry, and to my broken heart and mind brought renewal, joy, and Shalom. *Surprised by Agape is* a way of expressing gratitude to The Creator for how good and loving He has been to me. I also wrote this book for people of different worldviews, people that have experienced depression, loss, suicide; people that love life, music, literature, art, sports, history, philosophy, theology, or whatever interests them. In short, I wrote this for anyone who really wants a good read.

This book has taken many years to write, has been very hard work, and a labor of love. I want to say thanks to Dr. Don King, Rev Bill Barrow, the Scotsman David Jack, Douglas Gresham, Jonathan Atkinson, Jerry Root, Grant

Hudson of Clarendon House Publications, Kevin Jenson, Father Gary Ball, Carolyn Curtis, Andrew Jackson, Ryan Woodring, and everyone that has supported me, encouraged me, loved me, and who is part of my community. I want to end this book with a poem by George MacDonald that comes from his book *Diary of An Old Soul* which was published in 1880:

Take from me leisure, all familiar places;
Take all the lovely things of earth and air.
Take from me books; take all my precious faces;
Take words melodious, and their songful linking;
Take scents, and sounds, and all thy outsides fair;
Draw nearer, taking, and, to my sober thinking,
Thou bring'st them nearer all, and ready to my prayer.

Annotated Bibliography

Duriez, Colin. *Lewis A Biography of Friendship*. Oxford, England: Lion Hudson, 2013.

This biography on Lewis by Colin Duriez explores the spiritual journey of Lewis from atheism to theism to Christianity, loss of his mother at a young age, his horrific experience in the First World War, becoming a student at Oxford, his friendship with J. R. R. Tolkien, Charles Williams, Hugo Dyson, Owen Barfield, cultural impact, and how he came to be one of the most renowned Christian apologists of the 20th century.

Duriez, Colin. *The Oxford Inklings: Lewis, Tolkien, And Their Circle*. Oxford, England: Lion Hudson, 2015.

This fascinating scholarly book by writer Colin Duriez on Lewis, J. R R. Tolkien, Charles Williams, Owen Barfield, and the Inklings explores the impact each writer had on one another, their impact on culture, academia, and very important biographical facts about their lives that shaped their worldview.

'(https://www.pdxmonthly.com/articles/2009/12/17/christo- pher-hitchens).

King, Don. *Yet One More Spring A Critical Study of Joy Davidman*. Grand Rapids, Michigan. Cambridge, U.K.: Wm.B. Eerdman's Publishing Company, 2015.

This is a scholarly work on the life and writings of Lewis's wife Joy Davidman. It explores her Jewish background, her brilliance as a writer, how she converted from communism and agnosticism to Christianity, and married Lewis.

Lewis, *An Experiment in Criticism.* Cambridge University Press. Cambridge, U.K. 1961

This book by Lewis is his approach to literary criticism. Lewis makes a distinction between those individuals who read books just once, and those who read them again and again. He calls the individuals who re-read, the 'literary.' Lewis admits that though music, literature and art is subjective, there is still a great difference in individuals whose lives are changed by works of art, and those individuals that read a book or listen to music because they need some sort entertainment to pass the time.

Lewis, *The Four Loves.* Harper Collins. New York, New York, 1960.

This book by Lewis that was originally radio broadcast given in 1958, is about the four Greek loves of affection, friendship, eros, and charity in the context of a Christian worldview.

Lewis, *George MacDonald: An Anthology.* Edited and with a preface by Lewis. Harper Collins. New York, New York. 2001

This book by Lewis is a selection of passages from George Mac- Donald's sermons, fantasy works, fairy tales, and novels. MacDonald was Lewis's favorite writer; he referred to him as his 'master.' When Lewis was a young atheist at the age of 16, he discovered George MacDonald's book fantasy work *Phantastes* and said that it 'baptised his imagination.' Lewis refers and quotes George MacDonald in many of his books. In order to really understand C. S. Lewis it is necessary to read MacDonald.

Lewis, A Grief Observed. New York, New York: Harper Collins.1996.

This poignant book is C.S. Lewis grieving over the loss of his wife Joy Davidman. Joy went into remission from bone cancer when Lewis's friend and Anglican priest Peter Bide laid hands on her. The next four years were the happiest years that Jack Lewis and Joy Davidman had together. The bone cancer eventually came back and took Joy's life. This is perhaps Lewis's most honest book. It is a raw and honest account of him going through anger, asking questions, and having his faith sustained by the grace of Christ in the midst of horrific suffering.

Lewis, The Great Divorce: A Dream. Harper Collins: New York, New York. 1946.

This work of fiction explores the impact of our decisions in the context of eternity. Lewis wrote George MacDonald as the sage guide, like Virgil is the guide for Dante in *The Divine Comedy.* Through each character in this fantasy work, Lewis is exploring issues about sin, salvation, heaven, and hell.

Lewis, Image and Imagination. Edited by Walter Hooper. Cambridge, United Kingdom: Cambridge University Press, 2013.

This book, edited by Walter Hooper, and published in 2013, is a selection of Lewis's essays on literature, literary criticism, book re- views, and essays on other themes.

Lewis, Letters of Lewis. Edited by W. H. Lewis and Walter Hooper New York, New York: Harper Collins 1966.

This volume of letters by Lewis, published in 1966, is edited by his secretary Walter Hooper, his brother Warren Lewis, and has a biographical foreword by Warren Lewis that gives insights into his brother Jack's life.

Lewis, Mere Christianity. New York, New York: Harper Collins, 2001.

This work of apologetics by Lewis was first originally radio broadcast during the Second World War. The talks were compiled in a book in 1952. It is a theological argument about the morality of a moral law that transcends time and culture, that Jesus is the same Jesus of faith and history, that reason and faith are not mutuality exclusive, and is also about pride, prayer, and the theological virtues of faith, hope, and love.

Lewis, On Joy. Edited by Lesley Walmsley. Nashville, Tennessee: Thomas Nelson, 1998.

This book has selections from many of Lewis's books about the mystical experiences he called 'Joy' that led him from atheism, to theism, to Christianity.

Lewis, Perelandra. New York: New York: Scribner, 2003.

This is the second book in C. S Lewis's Space Trilogy. It is set on the planet Venus. The main character, the philologist Ransom, is modeled on Lewis's friend J. R. R. Tolkien. In this book the planet Venus has just been created, and Ransom is up against his old colleague Weston, who has now become Satan incarnate. The Un-man tries to tempt the Green Lady, the mother of the planet, through philosophical debate, and it is up to Ransom to defeat the evil Un-man, save the planet, and help unite the Green Lady with the King of Perelandra.

Lewis, Poems. New York, New York.: Harper Collins, 1964.

This collection of Lewis's poems is edited by Walter Hooper and was originally published in 1964.

Lewis, A Preface to Paradise Lost. Oxford University Press: London, 1967.

This book by Lewis was a series of lectures given at a university in Wales about the theology in John Milton's Paradise Lost, and literary criticism.

Lewis, Preparing for Easter: Fifty Devotional Readings from Lewis compiled by Michael Maudlin. Harper Collins: New York, New York. 2017.

This Easter devotional book has 50 readings from the letters, poetry, fiction, and apologetics works from Lewis, beginning with Ash Wednesday, through Lent, to Easter.

Lewis, Surprised by Joy: The Shape of My Early Life. New York, New York: Harper Collins, 1955.

This autobiography by Lewis is about his childhood in Northern Ireland, the loss of his mother, his horrific experiences in the First World War, how he became a scholar of literature, and his journey from atheism, to theism, to Christianity.

Lewis, Studies in Words. Cambridge, United Kingdom: Cambridge University Press, 1960.

This book of literary criticism on the use of words by Lewis was originally given as lectures at Cambridge University.

Lewis, The World's Last Night: And Other Essays. New York, New York: Mariner Books, 2012

This is a series of essays by Lewis on prayer, the second coming of Christ, Screwtape proposing a toast, what good work and good art is, and other themes.

Lewis, Yours, Jack: Spiritual Direction from Lewis. Edited by Paul F. Ford. New York, New York: Harper Collins, 2008.

This is a selection of letters by Lewis from the years 1916 to 1963.

Phantastes: A Faerie Romance for Men and Women. George MacDonald. Peabody, Massachusetts: Hendrickson Publishers Marketing, 2011.

This fantasy work, written by George MacDonald in 1858, describes the adventures the character Anodos has in fairy land that shape him spiritually. It is a fascinating book with elements from Celtic mythology and Christian theology. This book had a profound impact on Lewis when was a young 16-year-old atheist. He said it 'baptised his imagination.'

Further Bibliography

Duriez, Colin. *C. S. Lewis A Biography of Friendship*. Oxford, Eng- land: Lion Hudson, 2013.

Duriez, Colin. The *Oxford Inklings: Lewis, Tolkien, And Their Circle*. Oxford, England: Lion Hudson, 2015.

Glaspey, Terry. *Not A Tame Lion: The Spiritual Legacy of C. S. Lewis*. Nashville, Tennessee: Cumberland Publishing House, 1996.

King, Don: Yet *One More Spring A Critical Study of Joy Davidman*. Cambridge, U. K: Wm. B. Eerdmans's Publishing Com- pany, 2015.

Lewis, C. S. *The Abolition of Man*. New York, NY: Harper Collins,1944.

------. *The Chronicles of Narnia*. New York, NY: Harper Collins, 2001.

------. *An Experiment in Criticism*. Cambridge, U. K: Cambridge Uni- versity Press,1961.

------. *The Discarded Image: An Introduction to Medieval and Renaissance Literature*. Cambridge, U. K.: Cambridge University Press, 1964.

Essay Collection; Faith, Christianity, and the Church. Edited by Lesley Walmsley. London, U. K.: Harper Collins, 2002.

------. *George MacDonald: An Anthology*. Edited and with a preface by C. S. Lewis. Harper New York: Harper Collins, 2001.

------. *The Great Divorce*. New York, NY: Harper Collins, 1946.

------. *A Grief Observed*. Introduction by Douglas Gresham. New York, NY: Harper Collins,1961.

------. *Image and Imagination*. Edited by Walter Hooper. Cambridge, United Kingdom: Cambridge University Press, 2013.

------. *The Letters of C. S. Lewis*. Edited by W. H. Lewis and Walter Hooper. Harper Collins: New York, NY, 1966.

------. *Mere Christianity*. New York, NY: Harper Collins, 1952.

------. *A Mind Awake: An Anthology of C. S. Lewis*. Edited by Clyde S. Kilby. New York, NY: Harper Collins, 1968.

------. *Miracles*. New York, NY: Harper Collins,1947.

------. *Perelandra*. New York: New York: Scribner, 2003.

------. *Preparing for Easter: Fifty Devotional Readings from C. S. Lewis* compiled by Michael G. Maudlin. New York, New York: Harper Collins, 2017.

------. *A Preface to Paradise Lost*. Oxford, U. K.: Oxford University Press, 1942.

------. *Poems*. New York, NY: Harper Collins, 1964.

------. *Reflections On The Psalms*. Orlando, Florida: Harcourt, 1958.

------. *Studies in Words*. Cambridge, United Kingdom: Cambridge University Press, 1967.

------. *Surprised by Joy: The Shape of My Early Life*. New York, NY: Harper Collins, 1955.

------. *Till We Have Faces*. Orlando, Florida: Harcourt Inc, 1956.

------. *The Weight of Glory: And Other Addresses.* New York, NY: Harper Collins,1949.

------. *The World's Last Night And Other Essays.* New York, NY: Mariner Books, 2012.

------. *Yours, Jack: Spiritual Direction from C. S. Lewis.* Edited by Paul F. Ford: New York, New York. HarperCollins, 2008.

MacDonald, George. *Phantastes*: *A Faerie Romance for Men and Women.* Marketing Pea-body, Massachusetts: Hendrickson Publishers, 2011.

Walmsley, Leslie. *C. S. Lewis On Joy.* Nashville, Tennessee: Thomas Nelson, 1998.

SURPRISED BY MYTH
A Collection of Essays on the Inklings and Friends

co-authored by
Justin Wiggins and Grant P. Hudson

This new book *Surprised by Myth*, a collaboration between Justin Wiggins and Grant Hudson, is a remarkable piece of work. It stands apart from most other works of its kind, if indeed there are any, in that both Justin and Grant each take their own viewpoint about the complex writings and attitudes of my Stepfather C. S. Lewis, and write their feelings and ideas about the work and indeed the man himself accordingly. To our benefit, this results in all of us being able to see differing angles on Lewis's ways of writing, and why both these two men (and anyone else) can read his works from very different background ideologies.

These two writers demonstrate (although they may not have meant to) that the writings of C. S. Lewis spread a broad variable (and valuable) depth of knowledge in his books that is almost instantly understood by anyone who reads this book of their carefully studied works. There is deep value in this, as you will find, when you read *Surprised by Myth*.

Douglas Gresham, step-son of C. S. Lewis and author of *Lenten Lands: My Childhood with Joy Davidman and C.S. Lewis*.

Bringing together both spirit and matter as they are meant to be, Wiggins and Hudson offer wisdom and clarity through these broad-ranging essays. With an insider's eye, and as lovers of myth, these authors bring us ever closer to the heart and mind of the Inklings. A do not miss for anyone who reads Lewis, Tolkien and the Inklings.

Patti Callahan, NYT bestselling author of *Becoming Mrs. Lewis.*

The delight of reading this book is that it takes you into a world of discovery from two literary explorers, Grant P. Hudson and Justin Wiggins, who vibrantly merge their insights. Their vision is heightened in living through the grim new normal of the global grip of Covid in the last two years. Their vision freshly discovers the power of myth, fantasy and imaginative thought as an active dimension of rediscovered truth and hope. The reader is caught up in their shared vision, drawn from a well-chosen selection of the Inklings, and others.

Colin Duriez, author of *The Oxford Inklings: Lewis, Tolkien and Their Circle*

Surprised by Myth, co-authored by Justin Wiggins and Grant Hudson, is a fascinating collection of personal essays focused upon C. S. Lewis, J. R. R. Tolkien, and other Inklings related writers and friends. Each essay delves into how either Wiggins or Hudson has been profoundly influenced by the mythopoeic writings they consider. There is a fresh, honest candor in their approach, and each is deeply thankful for how their lives have been enriched through their encounters with myth, truth, and the One who is beyond all time. Readers will find much to enjoy and much to muse upon later. In their own modest ways, Wiggins and Hudson invite readers to go "further up and further in!"

Don King, C.S.Lewis scholar & Professor of Literature at Montreat College, author of *Yet One More Spring A Critical Study of Joy Davidman.*

Reading these essays is like participating in scintillating conversations that you'll want to experience again and again. To stimulate the conversations, the authors pose thought-provoking ideas mined from the literary genius of C. S. Lewis, J. R. R. Tolkien, and their circle of friends. These well-crafted essays not only offer a cornucopia of new perspectives and insights, but also enhance the meaning and understanding of classic myths, stories, and advice from some of the 20th century's most celebrated authors.

Steven A. Beebe, Ph.D. Regents' and University Distinguished Professor Emeritus, Texas State University, author of *C. S. Lewis and the Craft of Communication*

Surprised by Myth is a rich and varied offering from Messers Wiggins and Hudson. Their delight in the Inklings is clear, their knowledge deep, and (especially pleasing, this) they have widened the circle of their appeal to include Sayers, Chesterton, and the "father of the Inklings" himself, my countryman George MacDonald.

David Jack, translator of Scots to English George MacDonald novels

When we consider art and reality and how they relate to one another, we might ask what is true, what is truest. In the finite world, however, the better question might be to ask what is it art and reality reveal to us. In a delightful blend of personal and academic essays, Wiggins and Hudson explore those very questions as they discuss the universal and personal influence of myth.

Christine Norvell, author of *Till We Have Faces: A Reading Companion*

Imagine taking two friends out to lunch who are experts on Lewis and Tolkien? How much do you think it would cost you? For much less than the price of a meal with Justin Wiggins and Grant Hudson, you can read about their insights into Lewis and Tolkien and a lot more in *Surprised by Myth*. Justin and Grant provide "bite-size" thoughts in the form of short essays with a couple of rich desserts (in the form of two character studies) that will leave you satisfied and hungry for another meal with them.

William O'Flaherty creator of EssentialCSLewis.com, author of *The Misquotable C. S. Lewis* and *C.S. Lewis Goes to Hell*.

Personal accounts, including stories of redemption, make this new, insightful book a winner and a great tribute to C. S. Lewis and his dear friends. *Surprised by Myth* is a fine addition to the bookshelf of deep thinkers, literature lovers, and persons of faith."

Carolyn Curtis, author of *Women and C.S. Lewis: What His Life and Literature Reveal for Today's Culture*.

THE MYTH MAKERS

Essays on
C. S. Lewis and J. R. R. Tolkien

Grant P. Hudson

The Lion, the Witch and the Wardrobe was my favourite book as a child; then I discovered *The Lord of the Rings* and fell in love with its luminescence. It was a couple of years before I found out that the authors of both books were close friends and that Tolkien was a mentor of Lewis's. This set me off on a lifelong quest to explore their works.

In this volume I investigate the underlying purposes of each author: what makes Lewis's and Tolkien's work similar? What makes them different?

What key effect was each trying to create upon readers?

How did they accomplish those effects?

Examining such topics as the influence of Dante upon Lewis, the differing genres of his Space Trilogy, how Narnia developed, the role of allegory and symbolism, why some of their books succeed more than others, the principles of parallel universes, the influences on Tolkien including the Finnish national epic 'The Kalevala', the part played by metaphysics and language in Tolkien's creation of Middle-earth, recurring images, the role of Owen Barfield's work, and much, much more, this book was written for those who love Lewis and Tolkien and want to appreciate the real power and importance of what it was that they were accomplishing in the middle of the Twentieth Century and for generations since.

Grant P. Hudson is a published author and poet, with over 5,000 items of merchandise available featuring his artwork. He is the founder of Clarendon House Publications which has helped hundreds of authors from all over the world find a voice. His life-long passion for the works of Tolkien and Lewis led him into many adventures, including the development of theories of how fiction really works.

Join the
Inner Circle Writers' Group
on Facebook!

This group is unlike most writers' groups on social media.
Post ANYTHING about writing, including:
- passages from books you admire
- recommended reading
- extracts from your own work
- requests for advice or guidance about anything to do with writing

'Our little ICWG family is certainly a wonderful group full of kindness and encouragement. It's wonderful to see the growth of so many writers from the help and guidance they've received from this group alone'

Founded in 2008, this group is a thriving community, celebrating fiction of all kinds. Here you can also get a glimpse of the unique and revolutionary 'physics of fiction' as outlined in the book *How Stories Really Work* (see below) and in many articles and items. This is not available anywhere else.

The group is free and fun. Just go to Facebook:

https://www.facebook.com/groups/
innercirclewritersgroup

HOW STORIES REALLY WORK:
Exploring the Physics of Fiction
by Grant P. Hudson

Learn:
• what a story really is
• what it is actually doing to and for you and other readers
• the things called 'plots', what they are and how they are actually made
• the four categories of the powerful force that compels readers to turn pages
• the magnetic power that attracts readers even before the introduction of any character
• what the thing called a 'character' actually is, and how to rapidly build a convincing one
• what 'protagonists' and 'antagonists' really are, and what the connection between them consists of
• the 'nuclear reactor' that drives all successful stories through to their conclusion
• how the four basic genres - Epic, Tragedy, Irony and Comedy - are
composed and how they work to create different effects

and much, much more.

What the experts say:

As with all professionals, I too read craft books every day, to stay on top of my game. Over the last thirty years, I've read (literally) hundreds of writing books. And, lemme tell ya, the VAST majority of them are garbage. The relative few that are decent still aren't great. Writing instructors usually spend 60,000 words saying what could've been said in 60.

EXCEPT for yours, Grant. Your books are hands down, bar none, exceptional. You get down into the nitty gritty and talk about real stuff that's immediately useful. I especially like How Stories Really Work. You really nailed it with that one.

And, Grant... it's REALLY hard to impress me. But, you had me hooked from the very first sentence. In fact, I've already turned a number of my past clients onto it.

So... thank you for giving the writing world something of merit. Your book is a breath of invigorating fresh air. May it breathe new life into this great industry of ours so that writers may once again set the world on fire.

-J. C. Admore, Professional Writing Expert

An amazing book. Fascinating application of physics theory to the art of fiction writing. Presents new ways of understanding how stories work. I now look for 'vacuums' everywhere. Excellent case studies covering all genres. Thought-provoking and inspiring. I highly recommend this book to all readers and writers of fiction.

- G. Leyland (B Social Work, Grad Dip Writing, MA Creative Writing)

What the authors say:

I'm reading through How Stories Really Work. I've studied writing books for years but I've never seen anything like this!

I learned about your work after reading an article you wrote. I was intrigued by the premise, but at the time, there wasn't an Amazon review (something I must rectify when I'm finished). I decided it wouldn't hurt to read the preview. . . And promptly bought it.

This book is REVOLUTIONARY. Everything is made so simple and precise that other methods of writing seem clumsy by comparison. It's not just a way of writing, but a way of seeing.

-A. P. (Author)

It's beautiful, informative, essential reading for anyone who wants to write fiction. It's almost a responsibility point, you're committing a crime if you don't get it into peoples' hands!!!

-B.R. (Author)

Loved the book. Have used the principles in many a story. It all makes so much sense. If you want help in drawing readers in - this is the book to get.

-M W-B (Author)

This is a book every author should own. Grant P. Hudson does an outstanding job explaining story structure and the mechanics involved in creating a story or novel that readers will love. His examples are explained in an engaging manner so this book doesn't seem like reading a text book. I have already implemented many of his ideas in building a novel. This book contains great advice and I highly recommend it to all authors.
-D. T. (Author)

After reading this book, I'll never look at stories the same way. This step-by-step how-to book is full of wisdom about how classic stories are structured. You will see how to apply these principles to your own stories and novels, converting them to page-turners.

-P. V. A. (Author)

An essential purchase for anyone wishing to not only improve their writing but understand the art of story telling. You will never read a book the same way again. Nor watch a film or play without seeing the theory, that Grant so eloquently describes. Brilliant, worth every penny.

-D. S. (Author)

I have had nearly 100 short stories published and thought I knew about writing. This book taught me new ways to look at my own writing as well as other writing. Grant Hudson doesn't recycle old ways to look at the writing process, he invents new ways for a writer to examine almost every aspect of writing fiction, and provides a new vocabulary for how to do it. Very highly recommended for anyone who writes or wants to write fiction.

-A. C. (Author)

I wish I had found this book sooner. It was fascinating and insightful. I am now very annoying when watching films as I apply the techniques learned in this book, and quickly guess the twists! Very helpful in planning and forming ideas and I use this technique when writing stories.

-S. C. (Author)

I love the way Grant has approached the whole subject in this excellent book, in a very different and almost 'obvious' way compared to other books that attempt to teach the craft of writing. As a writer myself I now see in a different light what I am writing. Where was this book 35 years ago when I first started writing? One of those 'I wish I'd known that years ago' books.

-J. W. F. (Author)

I finished this book over two nights and had an epiphany. Such common sense and thought provoking ideas. This should be a mandatory text book for any serious writer. I'm excited to inject more purpose to my writing. This book will become a constant reference book for me now. Highly recommend it.

-R. C. (Author)

Your book is teaching me all the stuff that the other books don't! I can learn all about three-act structures and all that stuff elsewhere -this book is telling me exactly what to put INTO the structure! It makes writing so easy and you can immediately spot where you're going wrong! Excellent!

-L.J. (Professional)

This is an absolutely amazing achievement! I highly recommend it to anyone interested in writing fiction.

-T.R. (Student)

I was extremely impressed. This is not idle flattery. You've done a superb job in uncovering the factors that go into making a great piece of literature.

-B.R. (Executive)

Printed in Great Britain
by Amazon

57037578R00079